THE ULTIMATE

EMERIL LAGASSE

Power AirFryer 360 Plus ™

COOKBOOK

2023

**The Most Comprehensive Guide to Mastering
Your Multicooker.**

*Steaming, Air Frying, Grilling and Searing Your Favorite
Meals in No Time!*

Book writing: Cookbook Academy Staff

Interior and Cover Designer: Laura Antonioli
Editor: Matt Smith
Production Manager: LP Business & Management LTD
Production Editor: Ash Rowling
Photography © 2020/2021: Janet Specter

COOKBOOK ACADEMY 2021 - by Ciro Russo

Given the great success of our publications, here are the links to other books written by us:

The Ultimate Ninja Foodi Cookbook 2021 - https://www.amazon.com/dp/B0914MSRH1
Pilot Kitchen - https://www.amazon.com/dp/B08TY8D66N

Table of Contents

Introduction • 1

Breakfast • 12

Poultry • 31

Vegetables and Side Dishes • 50

Appetizer • 70

Cakes, Cookies and Muffins • 89

Beef Dishes • 107

Bread, Bagel, and Pizza • 125

Pork Dishes • 136

Fish and Seafood Dishes • 154

Meatless Dishes • 172

Holiday Recipe • 190

Lamb and Goat Dishes • 208

Conclusion • 224

Introduction

In recent years, air fryers have become extremely popular.

They're popular with customers because they're lightweight, flexible, and capable of handling even the most difficult recipes. Since they cook in the same way, air fryers are often compared to convection ovens.

On top of air fryers, there is normally only one heating element, while convection ovens have three.

The Emeril Lagasse Power Air Fryer 360 has five heating elements and a 1500-watt engine.

It has 12 cooking presets, a memory feature, an extra-large capacity, and a brushed stainless-steel body that is both elegant and durable.

If you're thinking of planning to get an air fryer, wait a little longer and learn why an air fryer oven might be a better option for you.

We all want to eat more nutritious foods, but we don't want to give up our favorite foods in the process!

The Emeril Lagasse Power Airfryer 360 does just that: allows you to cook, bake, roast, and more delicious meals right on your kitchen countertop—without the use of oils, fats, or grease.

This powerful countertop oven, which uses a 360° whirlpool of superheated air to cook your food, can replace up to nine different kitchen cooking accessories, such as a convection oven, toaster oven, and other appliances, thus lowering the number of calories by almost every meal!

How Does the Emeril Lagasse Power Air Fryer 360 Work?

The hot air created by the heating elements is used to cook the food in air fryers. Convection fans circulate hot air to cook the food uniformly on all sides, similarly to convection ovens.

For best results, the 5 heating elements of the Emeril Lagasse Power Air Fryer 360 will be activated by the device depending on the cooking function chosen.

Air fried, toast, pizza, broil, bake, bagel, rotisserie, dehydrate, roast, reheat, warm, and slow cook are among the 12 presets. Between the top and bottom heating elements, there are four levels where you can position your tray, rack, or pan while cooking. For easy reference, the guide is also printed on the glass door.

Broiling and dehydrating are best done in the first position, closest to the top heating element. Toast, bagel, broil, air fry, dehydrate, and rotisserie functions are all available in the second position. The reheat, bake, roast, steam, pizza, and dehydrate functions are all found in the third position. Finally, the slow cook feature is found in the fourth position.

Programs and Functions

Air fry

The air fry feature will use the side heating elements for operation, with the air fry fans switched on. In the second location, position the crisper tray. It's better to use the baking tray and pizza rack just below the crisper tray while cooking foods with enough moisture or fat content that may drip during the cooking process.

Toast

To make those toasted brown colorations on both sides, the toast feature uses the top and bottom heating elements. From one to five, you can choose how dark your toast should be. It can toast six slices of loaf bread at once.

Bagel

The top and bottom heating elements are used in the bagel feature, while the air frying fans are switched off. You can fit up to six slices of bagels and choose the toast's darkness, just like with the toast feature. When this function is used, the pizza rack is moved to the second position.

Pizza

The top and bottom heating elements are used for the pizza function. The bottom heating unit crisps the dough, while the top heats the toppings and melts the cheese. During the cooking process, the air frying fans can be turned on.

Bake

The bake feature uses the top and bottom heating elements and allows you to switch on or off the air frying fans, it is ideal for baking pastries, cakes, and pies.

Broil

Broiling and melting cheeses over burgers, sandwiches, or fries is easy with the broil function. While the air frying fan is turned off, it uses the top heating element. To get the best results, the pizza rack should be positioned near the top heating part.

Rotisserie

The top and bottom heating components, as well as the revolving spit accessory, are used in the rotisserie function. Food turns brown and crispy on the outside while remaining sweet and juicy on the inside.

Slow cook

The top and bottom heating elements are used in the slow cook function. It works well with a Dutch oven, the baking dish with lid, or any other similar cooking pot for making tender pulled pork or beef brisket. The Power Air Fryer 360 can cook for up to 10 hours on "slow cooking" mode.

Roast

The roast feature is the better preset for cooking large cuts of meat since it equally cooks the meat on all sides. It also makes use of the heating elements on the top and bottom.

Dehydrate

Fruits, vegetables, and meat can all be dried using the dehydrate feature. To uniformly dry out the ingredients, it only uses the top heating element with the air frying fans switched on during the process.

Reheat

With the option to switch on the air frying fans, the reheat mechanism uses both the top and bottom heating components. It's perfect for reheating food that doesn't need to be seared.

Warm

With the air frying fans turned off, the warm mechanism uses the top and bottom heating elements. It's perfect for keeping food at a comfortable temperature until you're ready to serve it.

Benefits of Air Fryer Oven Cooking

Compact and versatile

Air fryer ovens, unlike traditional ovens, can comfortably fit on your kitchen countertop and be stored when not in use. They're adaptable and can do a variety of tasks in the kitchen.

Energy-efficient

Air fryer ovens heat up and cook 40% faster than bulky, regular ovens.

Rotisserie function

It allows you to easily cook a whole chicken, a leg of lamb, a big chunk of beef, or multiple kebabs. Some air fryer ovens have a rotisserie spit or drum, which makes roasting meat or other foods a breeze.

Bigger capacity than standard air fryers

The interior has several layers, allowing you to cook several foods at the same time. A whole chicken can be cooked in under an hour using just the Power Air Fryer 360.

Requires much less oil than traditional cookers

Air fryers use 70% less oil than regular deep fryers, making them a more cost-effective and healthier option.

Easy to clean

Stainless steel or aluminum are used in the majority of air fryer toast ovens. They are not only fashionable and beautiful, but they are also long-lasting and food-safe. The cooking chamber and removable parts are normally made of stainless steel or coated with a non-stick coating. The oven racks, air fry baskets, and other accessories are also dishwasher-safe.

Tips for Cooking Success

- Before using the appliance, make sure you complete the necessary initial steps.

- Foods with a smaller size will take less time to prepare. Cutting food into equal sizes will ensure easier and more even cooking, which will help you save time in the kitchen.

- A crispier texture can be achieved by spraying, misting, or gently brushing food with oil before cooking. Ensure that you don't add too much or it will get soggy.

- To achieve even cooking, turn or stir the food halfway through the cooking time.

- You can use the air fryer oven to make snack or pastry recipes that would normally be made in a conventional oven.

- Make sure the food isn't overcrowded. Allow some space between pans, particularly when cooking food with a coating or batter, to allow hot air to circulate and evenly cook the food.

- When making recipes that call for high temperatures, use oils with a high smoking point or that can withstand high temperatures. Avocado, peanut, and grapeseed oils are all good examples. The smoke point of olive oil is low. If you must use olive oil, use extra light olive oil, which has a higher smoke point and won't dry out the food until it finishes cooking.

- Do not put cooking trays or pans directly on the bottom heating elements, as this will prevent hot air from circulating properly and cooking the food.

- Oil and grease crumbs and drippings can cause smoke and burn. Place a baking tray lined with foil and parchment paper underneath the crisper tray or baking pan to avoid this.

Guidelines for Safety and Precautions

Reading the user manual is one of the first things you should do after getting your device. Not only will it advise you on the proper use, but it will also protect you from any accidents while using it.

For those of you who may have misplaced the instructions in the package (or for those who are simply a little distracted...) here are some of the guidelines to remember when using the Emeril Lagasse power air fryer.

DO

- This appliance is only meant to be used indoors.

- Only people with normal auditory, emotional, and physical abilities who have read and understood the manual should use the appliance.

- Keep out of wet areas and hot surfaces like stovetops.

- Place the air fryer oven on a counter or table that is stable, level, and heat-resistant.

- Leave at least five inches of clearance around the oven during service, as it can heat up and release steam.

- Once the oven is in operation, make sure there is no food protruding from it.

- When removing food from the oven, use oven mitts, gloves, or dish towels.

- Make sure the appliance is completely turned off before carefully unplugging it.

- After each use, unplug and clean the appliance.

- When the drip tray is halfway full, remove it and clean it.

- When removing any hot oil from the unit, use caution.

- Allow at least 30 minutes for the machine to cool fully after unplugging it.

DO NOT

- Use an extension cord with this appliance to prevent accidents.

- Use the unit without the drip tray installed.

- Place anything on top of the oven.

- Block the air vents, especially while the unit is turned on.

- Put flammable materials near or on top of the air fryer oven such as paper, plastic, curtains, towels, etc.

- Connect to an electrical outlet that is already used by other appliances as it may cause it to overload.

- Connect with an electrical outlet other than a 2-prong grounded 120V.

- Modify the plug or any part of the unit.

- Use accessories that are not recommended by the manufacturer.

- Clean parts with metal scouring pads and abrasive chemicals.

- Submerge the unit in water.

- Line the drip tray with foil.

- Use metal utensils or cutleries to prevent electric shock.

Follow the steps below when you are about to use the unit for the first time.

1. All packaging materials, labels, and stickers must be removed and properly disposed of before using your air fryer oven for the first time.

2. Use warm water and a mild detergent to clean the crisper tray, drip tray, pizza rack, baking pan, rotisserie spit, and rotisserie stand. Thoroughly dry the region.

3. With the aid of a moist cloth and a mild detergent, clean the exterior and interior. Make sure the fabric isn't too damp, as this could cause water to soak into some electrical components.

4. Connect the device to an outlet on the kitchen counter.

5. Burn off any protective coating or oil by preheating the oven for a few minutes. During this stage, it's common for some smoke to appear.

6. Turn the device off, unplug it, and allow it to cool fully. With a damp rag, wipe the interior and exterior once more.

Measurement Conversion

Often you'll come across a fantastic recipe that uses unfamiliar measurements, such as mL instead of cups. Conversion charts, whether metric, imperial, or gas label, come in handy in this case, assisting you in creating whatever recipe you want to try.

When cooking, it's a good idea to have a kitchen scale and a set of full measuring cups on hand to ensure that the ingredients are correctly measured.

Abbreviations for Cooking Measurements

When you're following a recipe, it's critical to know what the cooking abbreviations mean. When writing out recipes, many authors use shorthand, and if you don't know what it means, you may make a few mistakes.

Abbreviations for Imperial/Standard Measurement

lb = Pound
qt = Quart
tsp = Teaspoon
pt = Pint
Oz = Ounce
c = Cup
fl. Oz = Fluid ounce
gal = Gallon
Tbsp = Tablespoon (also TB, Tbl)

Abbreviations for Metric Measurement

kg = kilogram

g = grams

l = liter

mL = Milliliter

Liquid Ingredients vs. Dry Ingredients Measurement

When it comes to weighing, dry and liquid ingredients should be handled differently. Measuring cups and spoon sets are commonly used to measure dry ingredients, while liquid measuring cups are used to measure liquids. Exact measurements can be achieved by using the appropriate measuring instruments.

To get the most precise number when measuring dry ingredients, fill the cup to the brim and scrape the excess off the end. A liquid measuring cup cannot be used for this, which is why it should not be used. Although a liquid measuring cup will give you a more precise liquid measurement, when a recipe calls for small quantities of liquid, you will need to use measuring spoons instead.

These recommendations are particularly useful when preparing recipes that necessitate precise measurements.

Fluid Ounces vs Ounces

The difference between using ounces and fluid ounces comes down to the difference between liquid and dry ingredients. Weight is measured in ounces, while volume is measured in fluid ounces. Liquid ingredients are measured in fluid ounces, while dry ingredients are measured in ounces (by weight) (by volume). So just because a recipe calls for 8 ounces of flour doesn't mean you'll need 1 cup.

Most American recipes (using the standard/imperial system) would list dry ingredients in cups/tablespoons/etc. instead of ounces. Remember this when you're weighing your ingredients!

Basic Kitchen Conversions & Equivalents

In the kitchen, having a basic understanding of cooking measurements and conversions is important. When you're following a recipe, it's important to understand what everything means. You can't always find the darn tablespoon to measure out your ingredients, so you have to wing it... However, if you know that 1 tablespoon equals 3 teaspoons, you can weigh with confidence!

Simply follow these kitchen conversion charts, and you'll have them memorized in no time, just like your school's multiplication tables.

Conversion Chart for Dry Measurements.

3 teaspoons is equivalent to 1 tablespoon = 1/16 cup

6 teaspoons is equivalent to 2 tablespoons = ⅛ cup

12 teaspoons is equivalent to 4 tablespoons = ¼ cup

24 teaspoons is equivalent to 8 tablespoons = ½ cup

36 teaspoons is equivalent to12 tablespoons = ¾ cup

48 teaspoons is equivalent to16 tablespoons = 1 cup

Measurements Conversion Chart for Liquid

8 fluid ounces = 1 cup = ½ pint = ¼ quart

16 fluid ounces = 2 cups = 1 pint = ½ quart

32 fluid ounces = 4 cups = 2 pints = 1 quart = ¼ gallon

128 fluid ounces = 16 cups = 8 pints = 4 quarts = 1 gallon

Butter

1 cup butter = 2 sticks = 230 grams = 8 ounces = 8 tablespoons

Metric Cooking Measurement vs Standard Imperial Cooking Measurements

Metric to US Cooking Conversions

Oven Temperatures

- 120 c = 250 F
- 160 c = 320 F
- 180 c = 350 F
- 205 c = 400 F
- 220 c = 425 F

Baking in grams

- 1 cup heavy cream = 235 grams
- 1 cup sugar = 150 grams
- 1 cup powdered sugar = 160 grams
- 1 cup Flour = 140 grams

Volume

- 1 milliliter is equivalent to 1/5 teaspoon
- 5 ml is equivalent to 1 teaspoon
- 15 ml is equivalent to 1 tablespoon
- 240 ml is equivalent to 1 cup or 8 fluid ounces
- 1 liter is equivalent to 34 fl. ounces

Weight

- 1 gram = .035 ounces
- 100 grams = 3.5 ounces
- 500 grams = 1.1 pounds
- 1 kilogram = 35 ounces

US to Metric Cooking Conversions

- 1 pound = 454 grams
- 1 gallon (16 cups) = 3.8 liters
- 1 cup = 237 ml
- 1 tsp = 5 ml
- 1 tbsp = 15 ml
- 1 fl ounce = 30 ml
- 1 pint (2 cups) = 473 ml
- 1 quart (4 cups) = .95 liter
- 1 oz = 28 grams
- 1/5 tsp = 1 ml

What is 1 Cup Equivalent to?

Knowing what 1 cup equals is useful because, even if you don't have any kitchen measuring instruments, most people would have a 1 cup measurement. It can also be useful for cooking conversions while halving or doubling recipes. Just keep in mind that 1 cup equals these different measurements, so everything in this chart is equivalent!

- 1 cup = 8 fluid ounces
- 1 cup = 16 tablespoons
- 1 cup = 48 teaspoons
- 1 cup = ½ pint
- 1 cup = ¼ quart
- 1 cup = 1/16 gallon
- 1 cup = 240 ml

Baking Pan Conversions

(The cups denote the amount of batter that will fit into the pan.)

- 9-inch square pan = 8 cups
- 10-inch bundt pan = 12 cups
- 9 x 5 inch loaf pan = 8 cups
- 9-inch round cake pan = 12 cups
- 10-inch tube pan = 16 cups
- 9-inch springform pan = 10 cups

Conversion of Common Baking Measurements to Ounces

- 1 cup unsifted powdered sugar = 4.4oz
- 1 cup all-purpose flour = 4.5oz
- 1 cup rolled oats = 3oz
- 1 large egg = 1.7oz
- 1 cup milk = 8oz

- 1 cup heavy cream = 8.4oz

- 1 cup granulated sugar = 7.1oz

- 1 cup packed brown sugar = 7.75oz

- 1 cup vegetable oil = 7.7oz

- 1 cup butter = 8oz

Ratings

In all of our cookbooks you'll find a grade of evaluation on each individual recipe called "Ratings".

The "Ratings" goes from 1 to 5 stars and it is determined by the complexity of the dish and the time you'll need to prepare it.

1 star will indicate a very quick and easy meal, while 5 stars will be a more complex recipe with higher preparation time needed.

We wanted to offer you this method of evaluating on every dish in order to make it even easier for you to choose the most suitable recipes according to your time availability.

Cookbook Academy Team

Breakfast

Breakfast Casserole

Preparation time
5 MINUTES

Cooking time
15 MINUTES

Servings
6

Ratings

Ingredients

4 eggs, beaten

1 lb. Italian sausage, cooked and crumbled

1 cup tomato, diced

2 tablespoons heavy cream

2 teaspoons Italian seasoning

1/2 cup cheddar cheese, shredded

Nutritional Info

Calories: 182kcal

Carbs: 37.6g

Fat: 2g,

Protein: 5.3g

Directions

1. In a small baking pan, add all of the ingredients, finishing with the cheese.

2. Place inside the air fryer oven.

3. Choose air fry setting.

4. Air fry at 340 degrees F for 5 minutes.

Serving suggestion

Garnish with chopped parsley.

Tip

Check the eggs if they are done. If not, extend cooking time in the air fryer oven.

Toaster Strudel

Preparation time
5 MINUTES

Cooking time
5 MINUTES

Servings
6

Ratings

Ingredients

1 pack frozen toaster strudels

Nutritional Info

Calories: 180kcal
Carbs: 27g
Fat: 7g,
Protein: 2g

Directions

1. Add the toaster straddles to the air crisper tray.

2. Select air fry function.

3. For 5 minutes cook at 350 degrees F.

Serving suggestion

Let cool before serving.

Tip

Air fry only what you'll eat for breakfast.

Baked Oatmeal with Blueberry

 Preparation time
5 MINUTES

 Cooking time
15 MINUTES

 Servings
4

Ratings

Ingredients

1 egg
1 cup milk
1/2 teaspoon cinnamon
1 cup rolled oats
1/2 teaspoon baking powder
3/4 cup brown sugar
1/2 teaspoon nutmeg
1/4 cup blueberries, sliced

Nutritional Info

Calories: 160kcal
Carbs: 27g
Fat: 4g,
Protein: 5g

Directions

1. Mix egg and milk together thoroughly in a bowl.

2. Mix the remaining ingredients except blueberries in another bowl.

3. Pour mixture into a small baking pan.

4. Top with the egg mixture and with the sliced blueberries.

5. Set your air fryer oven to bake.

6. Bake at 320 degrees F for 10 to 15 minutes.

Serving suggestion

Garnish with blueberry slices.

Tip

Check the eggs if they are done. If not extend cooking time.

Zucchini Bread

Preparation time
15 MINUTES

Cooking time
40 MINUTES

Servings
4

Ratings

Ingredients

Dry

3 cups all-purpose flour
1 teaspoon baking powder
1 teaspoon baking soda
1 teaspoon allspice
1 teaspoon ground nutmeg
1 teaspoon ground cinnamon
Pinch salt

Wet

3 eggs, beaten
2-1/4 cup sugar
1 cup vegetable oil
2 cups zucchini, grated
1 teaspoon vanilla extract
1 cup walnuts, chopped

Nutritional Info

Calories: 114kcal
Carbs: 13.7g
Fat: 6.1g,
Protein: 2.2g

Directions

1. Mix the dry ingredients in a bowl.

2. Combine the wet ingredients in another bowl.

3. Blend the two together.

4. Pour mixture into a baking pan.

5. Add the baking pan to the air fryer oven.

6. Select bake function.

7. Bake at 320 degrees F for 30 to 40 minutes.

Serving suggestion

Serve with cream cheese.

Tip

Use mini loaf pan.

Egg Cups

Preparation time
5 MINUTES

Cooking time
10 MINUTES

Servings
2

Ratings

Ingredients

Cooking spray

2 eggs, beaten

1/4 cup milk

Salt and pepper to taste

2 slices bread

2 eggs

1/4 cup cheddar cheese, shredded

Nutritional Info

Calories: 59kcal

Carbs: 1g

Fat: 0g,

Protein: 12g

Directions

1. Spray your ramekins with oil.

2. In a bowl, mix the beaten eggs and milk.

3. Season with salt and pepper.

4. Dip the bread in this mixture.

5. Press bread onto the ramekins.

6. Crack eggs on top of bread. Sprinkle with cheese.

7. Place the ramekins inside the air fryer oven.

8. Choose air fry function.

9. Air fry at 330 degrees F for 7 minutes.

Serving suggestion

Garnish with chopped parsley.

Tip

Use whole-wheat bread.

Cheesy Hash Browns

Preparation time
10 MINUTES

Cooking time
10 MINUTES

Servings
4

Ratings

Ingredients

4 potatoes, grated
1/2 cup onion, chopped
1/2 cup cheddar cheese, grated
1 egg, beaten
3 teaspoons garlic powder
Salt and pepper to taste
Cooking spray

Nutritional Info

Calories: 129kcal
Carbs: 7.3g
Fat: 8.6g,
Protein: 5.6g

Directions

1. Mix the ingredients in a bowl.

2. Spray the air fryer tray with oil.

3. Add the mixture to the air crisper tray.

4. Choose air fry setting.

5. Air fry at 400 degrees F for 4 minutes.

6. Stir and cook for another 5 minutes.

Serving suggestion

Serve with eggs and sausages.

Tip

You can also cook frozen pre-prepared hash brown in the air fryer oven.

English Muffin Sandwich

 Preparation time
5 MINUTES

 Cooking time
5 MINUTES

 Servings
1

Ratings

Ingredients

Cooking spray
1 egg
1 English muffin, split in 2
2 slices bacon, cooked crispy

Directions

1. Spray our ramekin with oil.

2. Crack the egg inside the ramekin.

3. Add the ramekin to the air fryer basket.

4. Place the muffin beside.

5. Choose air fry function.

6. Air fry at 330 degrees F for 4 minutes.

7. Top the muffin with bacon slices and egg.

8. Top with the other muffin slice.

Serving suggestion

Serve with milk or coffee.

Tip

You can also use other types of bread for this recipe.

Avocado Toast

Ratings

Ingredients

1 avocado, mashed
1 clove garlic, minced
1 teaspoon lemon juice
Salt to taste
2 slices bread
Chopped tomatoes

Nutritional Info

Calories: 192.5kcal
Carbs: 26.7g
Fat: 4.6g,
Protein: 14.9g

Directions

1. Mix the mashed avocado, garlic, lemon juice, salt and pepper.

2. Spread avocado mixture on top of the bread slices.

3. Top with the tomatoes.

4. Choose air fry option.

5. Air fry at 330 degrees F for 3 minutes.

Serving suggestion

Sprinkle with pepper.

Tip

Use whole wheat bread.

Baby Pancake with Raspberry

Preparation time
10 MINUTES

Cooking time
10 MINUTES

Servings
2

Ratings

Ingredients

1/2 cup all-purpose flour
1/2 cup milk
1/8 cup butter
3 eggs, beaten
1/2 teaspoon vanilla extract
Cooking spray
1/2 cup raspberries

Nutritional Info

Calories: 343kcal
Carbs: 13g
Fat: 26.3g,
Protein: 13g

Directions

1. Mix the flour, milk, butter, eggs and vanilla in a bowl.

2. Spray your muffin pan with oil.

3. Pour the batter into the muffin cups.

4. Place the muffin pan inside the air fryer oven.

5. Set your air fryer oven to air fry.

6. Cook for 5 minutesat 320 degrees F.

7. If not fully cooked, cook for 2 to 3 more minutes.

8. Top with raspberries.

Serving suggestion

Serve with maple syrup.

Tip

You can also sprinkle with confectioners' sugar.

Pumpkin Pancake

Preparation time
5 MINUTES

Cooking time
5 MINUTES

Servings
8

Ingredients

1 cup all-purpose flour

1/2 cup pumpkin puree

1/2 teaspoon baking soda

1 teaspoon baking powder

2 tablespoon brown sugar

1 teaspoon ground cinnamon

1/2 teaspoon ground nutmeg

2 tablespoons vegetable oil

1 egg, beaten

3/4 cup buttermilk

1 teaspoon vanilla extract

Pinch salt

Nutritional Info

Calories: 128kcal

Carbs: 26.9g

Fat: 1.1g,

Protein: 5g

Directions

1. Mix all the ingredients in a bowl.

2. Spray a small baking pan with oil.

3. Put a portion of the batter into the pan.

4. Select air fry setting.

5. Cook at 300 degrees F for 3 minutes per side.

6. Do the same steps for the remaining batter.

Serving suggestion

Drizzle with melted butter before serving.

Tip

You can use canned pumpkin puree.

Avocado Eggs

Preparation time
5 MINUTES

Cooking time
10 MINUTES

Servings
2

Ratings

Ingredients

1 avocado, sliced and pitted

2 eggs

Salt and pepper to taste

Nutritional Info

Calories: 447kcal

Carbs: 17g

Fat: 37g,

Protein: 15g

Directions

1. Crack the egg into the avocado hole.

2. Add the avocado halves to the air fryer tray.

3. Turn to air fry option.

4. Cook at 400 degrees for 10 minutes.

5. Sprinkle with the salt and pepper.

Serving suggestion

Serve with toasted whole wheat bread.

Tip

You can also season with dried herbs.

Three Cheese Quiche

Preparation time
10 MINUTES

Cooking time
20 MINUTES

Servings
6

Ratings

Ingredients

1 package frozen pie crust

4 oz. mozzarella cheese, shredded

4 oz. Parmesan cheese, shredded

8 oz. cheddar cheese, grated and divided

6 eggs

1/2 cup milk

1/2 cup sour cream

Nutritional Info

Calories: 360kcal

Carbs: 4g

Fat: 31g,

Protein: 25g

Directions

1. Add mozzarella and Parmesan cheese on top of the pie crust.
2. Top with half of the cheddar cheese.
3. In a bowl, beat the eggs.
4. Stir in the milk and cream.
5. Pour mixture on top of the cheese.
6. Place the crust in the air fryer tray.
7. Set it to bake function.
8. Cook at 300 degrees F for 12 to 15 minutes.
9. Sprinkle the remaining cheddar on top.
10. Cook for another 5 minutes.

Serving suggestion

Let cool before slicing.

Tip

Use low-fat sour cream.

Spinach and Tomato Frittata

 Preparation time
5 MINUTES

 Cooking time
10 MINUTES

 Servings
2

Ratings

Ingredients

2 eggs

2 tablespoons milk

1 tablespoons Parmesan cheese, grated

Salt and pepper to taste

1/4 cup spinach, sliced

1/4 cup tomatoes, chopped

Nutritional Info

Calories: 186.2kcal

Carbs: 9.1g

Fat: 11.1g,

Protein: 11.9g

Directions

1. Beat the eggs in a bowl.

2. Stir in the milk, Parmesan cheese, salt and pepper.

3. Add the tomatoes and spinach.

4. Pour mixture into a baking pan.

5. Turn to air fry setting.

6. Air fry at 330 degrees F for 7 minutes.

Serving suggestion

Garnish with fresh basil leaves.

Tip

You can also use non-dairy milk for this recipe.

Bacon and Egg Cups

Preparation time
5 MINUTES

Cooking time
5 MINUTES

Servings
4

Ratings

Ingredients

4 pieces of Canadian bacon

4 eggs

Salt and pepper to taste

Nutritional Info

Calories: 111kcal

Carbs: 0.6g

Fat: 8.1g,

Protein: 8.2g

Directions

1. Line your muffin pan with bacon slices.

2. Crack eggs into each of the cups.

3. Add the muffin pan to the air fryer oven.

4. Set it to air fry.

5. Cook at 330 degrees F for 5 minutes.

Serving suggestion

Sprinkle with pepper before serving.

Tip

Use Canadian bacon for this recipe.

Broccoli Quiche

Preparation time
15 MINUTES

Cooking time
15 MINUTES

Servings
4

Ratings

Ingredients

4 eggs

2 cups broccoli florets

1 cup cheddar cheese, shredded

1-1/2 cup milk

Salt and pepper to taste

1 frozen pie crust

Nutritional Info

Calories: 235.5kcal

Carbs: 13g

Fat: 16g,

Protein: 10.4g

Directions

1. Combine the eggs, broccoli, cheese, milk, salt and pepper in a bowl.

2. On top of the pie crust pour the mixture.

3. Add the pie crust to the air fryer tray.

4. Choose air fry function.

5. Cook at 320 degrees F for 12 to 15 minutes.

Serving suggestion

Garnish with chopped parsley.

Tip

If eggs are not fully cooked after 15 minutes, reduce temperature to 300 degrees F and cook for another 5 minutes.

Sausage Patties

Preparation time
5 MINUTES

Cooking time
10 MINUTES

Servings
8

Ratings

Ingredients

1 package thawed sausage patties

Nutritional Info

Calories: 190kcal
Carbs: 0.5g
Fat: 18g,
Protein: 6g

Directions

1. Spread the sausage patties on the air fryer tray.
2. Set it to air fry.
3. For 5 minutes cook at 400 degrees F.
4. Flip and cook for another 5 minutes.

Serving suggestion

Garnish with parsley.

Tip

Thaw the sausages before air frying.

Breakfast Burrito

Preparation time
25 MINUTES

Cooking time
5 MINUTES

Servings
4

Ratings

Ingredients

4 scrambled eggs

1 lb. ground sausage, cooked and crumbled

1/2 cup red bell pepper, chopped

4 tortillas

1/2 cup salsa

1/2 cup cheese, shredded

Nutritional Info

Calories: 394.9kcal

Carbs: 19.5g

Fat: 25.1g,

Protein: 21.0g

Directions

1. Mix the eggs, sausage and red bell pepper.

2. Add this mixture on top of the tortillas.

3. Sprinkle with cheese.

4. Roll up the tortillas.

5. Select air fry option.

6. For 5 minutes cook at 400 degrees F.

7. Spread the salsa on top.

Serving suggestion

Garnish with basil leaves.

Tip

Use Colby Jack cheese for this recipe.

Chocolate French Toast

Preparation time
10 MINUTES

Cooking time
10 MINUTES

Servings
4

Ratings

Ingredients

4 eggs, beaten
1 cup milk
1/4 cup cocoa powder
1/2 cup sugar
1/2 teaspoon baking powder
Pinch salt
8 slices bread, cut into strips

Nutritional Info

Calories: 560kcal
Carbs: 92.1g
Fat: 17.8g,
Protein: 15.6g

Directions

1. Mix the eggs, milk, cocoa powder, sugar, baking powder and salt in a bowl.

2. Dip the bread slices in the mixture.

3. Let it soak for 5 minutes.

4. Transfer to the air fryer oven.

5. Choose toast setting.

6. For 5 minutes per side cook at 350 degrees F.

Serving suggestion

Dust with powdered sugar.

Tip

Use unsweetened cocoa powder.

Poultry

Ranch Chicken Wings

Preparation time
10 MINUTES

Cooking time
25 MINUTES

Servings
2

Ratings

Ingredients

1 lb chicken wings
2 tbsp butter, melted
1 1/2 tbsp ranch seasoning
1 tbsp garlic, minced

Nutritional Info

Calories 561
Fat: 28.4 g
Carbohydrates: 1.4 g
Sugar: 0.1 g
Protein: 66 g
Cholesterol: 232 mg

Directions

1. In a bowl, mix butter, garlic, and ranch seasoning.

2. Add chicken wings and toss to coat.

3. Put the bowl in the refrigerator overnight, covered.

4. Arrange marinated chicken wings in a crispier tray.

5. Place the drip tray below the bottom of the air fryer.

6. Insert the crispier tray into shelf position 4.

7. Select air fry mode. Set the temperature knob to 360 F and the timer for 25 minutes. Press start.

8. Turn chicken wings halfway through.

9. Serve and enjoy.

Lemon Pepper Chicken

Preparation time
10 MINUTES

Cooking time
15 MINUTES

Servings
6

Ratings

Ingredients

6 chicken thighs, skinless & boneless

1/2 tbsp lemon pepper seasoning

1 1/2 tbsp fresh lemon juice

1/2 tsp garlic powder

1/2 tsp Italian seasoning

1/2 tsp paprika

Pepper

Salt

Nutritional Info

Calories 282

Fat: 11 g

Carbohydrates: 0.7 g

Sugar: 0.2 g

Protein: 42.4 g

Cholesterol: 130 mg

Directions

1. Add chicken thighs into the bowl.

2. Add remaining ingredients and coat well.

3. Place chicken thighs in a crispier tray.

4. Place the drip tray below the bottom of the air fryer.

5. Insert the crispier tray into shelf position 4.

6. Select air fry mode. Set the temperature knob to 360 F and the timer for 15 minutes. Press start.

7. Serve and enjoy.

Jerk Wings

 Preparation time
10 MINUTES

 Cooking time
20 MINUTES

 Servings
2

Ratings

Ingredients

1 lb chicken wings
1 tbsp jerk seasoning
1 tsp olive oil
1 tbsp cornstarch
Pepper
Salt

Nutritional Info

Calories 466
Fat: 19.1 g
Carbohydrates: 3.7 g
Sugar: 0 g
Protein: 65.6 g
Cholesterol: 202 mg

Directions

1. In a bowl, add chicken wings.

2. Add remaining ingredients on top of chicken wings and toss well.

3. Add chicken wings in a crispier tray.

4. Place the drip tray below the bottom of the air fryer.

5. Insert the crispier tray into shelf position 4.

6. Select air fry mode. Set the temperature knob to 380 F and the timer for 20 minutes. Press start.

7. Turn chicken wings halfway through.

8. Serve and enjoy.

Greek Chicken Breast

Preparation time
10 MINUTES

Cooking time
25 MINUTES

Servings
4

Ratings
★ ★ ★

Ingredients

4 chicken breasts, skinless & boneless

1 tbsp olive oil

For rub:

1 tsp oregano

1 tsp thyme

1 tsp parsley

1 tsp onion powder

1 tsp basil

Pepper

Salt

Nutritional Info

Calories 312

Fat: 14.4 g

Carbohydrates: 0.9 g

Sugar: 0.2 g

Protein: 42.4 g

Cholesterol: 130 mg

Directions

1. Brush chicken breast with oil.

2. In a mixing bowl, incorporate all of the rub ingredients and rub all over the chicken breasts.

3. Place chicken in a crispier tray.

4. Place the drip tray below the bottom of the air fryer.

5. Insert the crispier tray into shelf position 4.

6. Select air fry mode. Set the temperature knob to 390 F and the timer for 25 minutes. Press start.

7. Turn chicken halfway through.

8. Serve and enjoy.

Tasty Chicken Tenders

 Preparation time
10 MINUTES

 Cooking time
16 MINUTES

 Servings
4

Ratings

Ingredients

1 lb chicken tenders
For rub:
1/2 tbsp dried thyme
1 tbsp garlic powder
1 tbsp paprika
1/2 tbsp onion powder
1/2 tsp cayenne pepper
Pepper
Salt

Nutritional Info

Calories 232
Fat: 8.7 g
Carbohydrates: 3.6 g
Sugar: 1 g
Protein: 33.6 g
Cholesterol: 101 mg

Directions

1. In a bowl, add all rub ingredients and mix well.

2. Add chicken tenders into the bowl and coat well.

3. Place chicken tenders in a crispier tray.

4. Place the drip tray below the bottom of the air fryer.

5. Insert the crispier tray into shelf position 4.

6. Select air fry mode. Set the temperature knob to 370 F and the timer for 16 minutes. Press start.

7. Turn chicken tenders halfway through.

8. Serve and enjoy.

Roasted Chicken

Preparation time
20 MINUTES

Cooking time
1 HOUR

Servings
4

Ratings

Ingredients

4 lb. whole chicken
Dry rub
½ cup paprika
¼ cup garlic powder
1/8 cup salt
¼ cup pepper
3 tablespoons onion powder
3 tablespoons ground cayenne pepper
3 tablespoons dried thyme
3 tablespoons dried oregano

Nutritional Info

Calories: 241
Fat: 12g
Carbs: 6g
Protein: 12g

Directions

1. Combine dry rub ingredients in a bowl.
2. Rub chicken using ¼ cup of the dry rub mixture.
3. Truss the whole chicken.
4. Attach it to the rotisserie spit.
5. Place inside the air fryer oven.
6. Choose rotisserie setting.
7. Cook at 350 degrees F for 1 hour.

Chicken with Veggies

 Preparation time
10 MINUTES

 Cooking time
15 MINUTES

 Servings
2

Ratings

Ingredients

Chicken
2 chicken breast fillets
2 tablespoons olive oil
1 tablespoon onion powder
1 tablespoon garlic powder
Salt and pepper to taste
Veggies
1 cup cherry tomatoes
2 teaspoons olive oil
1 cup arugula

Nutritional Info

Calories: 221
Fat: 12g
Carbs: 5g
Protein: 14g

Directions

1. Brush the chicken breast fillets with oil.

2. Season with salt, pepper, onion powder, and garlic powder.

3. Place in the air crisper tray.

4. Select air fry function.

5. Cook at 370 degrees F for 4 to 5 minutes per side.

6. Transfer to a plate.

7. Toss the tomatoes in the olive oil.

8. Add to the air fryer tray.

9. Air fry at 350 degrees F for 5 minutes.

10. Serve the chicken with the arugula on the side topped with the roasted tomatoes.

Szechuan Chicken

Preparation time
20 MINUTES

Cooking time
10 MINUTES

Servings
2

Ratings

Ingredients

Chicken
1 lb. chicken breast fillet, diced
¼ cup cornstarch
Cooking spray
Sauce
¼ teaspoon garlic powder
1 tablespoon brown sugar
1 tablespoon black bean sauce
¼ cup mayonnaise
1 teaspoon hoisin
2 teaspoon honey
1 teaspoon rice wine vinegar
1 teaspoon ground Sichuan
Peppercorns

Nutritional Info

Calories: 240
Fat: 12g
Carbs: 4g
Protein: 12g

Directions

1. Combine the sauce ingredients in a bowl. Set aside.

2. Coat the diced chicken with cornstarch.

3. Spray with oil.

4. Place in the air crisper tray.

5. Set it to air fry.

6. Cook at 350 degrees F for 8 to 10 minutes, turning once.

7. Toss diced chicken in sauce and serve.

Korean Fried Chicken

 Preparation time
10 MINUTES

 Cooking time
10 MINUTES

 Servings
4

Ratings

Ingredients

Chicken
¼ cup water
¼ cup flour
Salt and pepper to taste
1 lb. chicken thigh fillet, diced
Cooking spray
Sauce
3 teaspoons gochujang
1 tablespoon sugar
1 tablespoon vinegar

Nutritional Info

Calories: 240
Fat: 12g
Carbs: 6g
Protein: 9g

Directions

1. Mix the water, flour, salt and pepper.

2. Dip chicken in the batter.

3. Spray with oil.

4. Choose air fry setting.

5. Cook at 350 degrees F for 5 to 7 minutes per side.

6. Mix the sauce ingredients.

7. Coat chicken with sauce before serving.

Cajun Chicken

Preparation time
10 MINUTES

Cooking time
20 MINUTES

Servings
6

Ratings

Ingredients

6 chicken drumsticks
Cooking spray
Cajun dry rub
1 teaspoon onion powder
½ teaspoon garlic powder
1 teaspoon paprika
½ teaspoon cayenne pepper
½ teaspoon dried thyme
½ teaspoon dried oregano
½ teaspoon dried basil
Salt and pepper to taste

Directions

1. Combine dry rub ingredients.

2. Spray chicken with oil.

3. Sprinkle all sides with Cajun seasoning.

4. Place these in the air crisper tray.

5. Cook each side at 400 degrees F for 10 minutes.

Nutritional Info

Calories: 227
Fat: 12g
Carbs: 4g
Protein: 9g

Paprika Chicken

 Preparation time
10 MINUTES

 Cooking time
30 MINUTES

 Servings
6

Ratings

Ingredients

2 lb. chicken wings
2 tablespoons olive oil
1 tablespoon paprika
1 teaspoon garlic powder
Salt and pepper to taste

Nutritional Info

Calories: 252
Protein: 29g
Fat: 15g
Carbs: 2g

Directions

1. Toss the chicken in olive oil.

2. Season with the paprika, garlic powder, salt and pepper.

3. Place in the air crisper tray.

4. Set the air fryer oven to air fry function.

5. Set the temperature to 400 degrees F.

6. Cook for 15 minutes per side.

Stuffed Chicken

Preparation time
10 MINUTES

Cooking time
20 MINUTES

Servings
2

Ratings

Ingredients

4 oz. garlic and herb cream cheese

2 chicken breast fillets

1 tablespoon olive oil

Pinch dried Italian herbs

Salt and pepper to taste

Nutritional Info

Calories: 253

Protein: 29g

Fat: 16g

Carbs: 4g

Directions

1. To make a pouch, cut a slit in the middle of the chicken breast.

2. Stuff the pocket with cream cheese.

3. Brush both sides with olive oil.

4. Season with Italian herbs, salt and pepper.

5. Set the stuffed chicken in the air crisper tray.

6. Cook at 370 degrees F for 10 minutes.

7. Flip and cook for another 10 minutes.

Lime Chicken

Preparation time
10 MINUTES

Cooking time
30 MINUTES

Servings
6

Ratings

Ingredients

1 tablespoon water

2 tablespoons lime juice

1 teaspoon lime zest

2 tablespoons chipotle in adobo sauce

Salt and pepper to taste

2 lb. chicken wings

Nutritional Info

Calories: 220

Fat: 14g

Carbs: 5g

Protein: 12g

Directions

1. Combine the water, lime juice, lime zest, chipotle in adobo sauce, salt and pepper.

2. Soak chicken wings in the sauce.

3. Coat evenly.

4. Place the chicken wings in the air crisper tray.

5. Cook at 380 degrees F for 12 minutes per side.

6. Increase temperature to 400 degrees F and cook for another 6 minutes.

Sesame Chicken

Preparation time
15 MINUTES

Cooking time
20 MINUTES

Servings
4

Ratings

Ingredients

1 lb. chicken thigh fillets, diced

½ cup potato starch

Sauce

2 tablespoons brown sugar

¼ cup soy sauce

2 tablespoons orange juice

¼ cup hoisin sauce

1 teaspoon ground ginger

1 teaspoon garlic powder

1 tbs cornstarch with 1 tbs water added

Nutritional Info

Calories: 220

Fat: 12g

Carbs: 5g

Protein: 13g

Directions

1. Cover chicken with potato starch.

2. Place chicken in the air crisper tray.

3. For 7 minutes per side cook at 350 degrees F.

4. Add the sauce ingredients except cornstarch mixture to a pan over medium heat.

5. Simmer for 3 minutes.

6. Stir in the cornstarch mixture.

7. Simmer for another 3 minutes.

Fried Frozen Chicken Tenderloins

 Preparation time
30 MINUTES

 Cooking time
25 MINUTES

 Servings
6

Ratings

Ingredients

Southern fried chicken tenderloins

Nutritional Info

Calories: 110kcal
Carbs: 0g
Fat: 1g,
Protein: 13g

Directions

1. Place the chicken in the crisper tray and place it on the highest rack holder.

2. Select the air fry setting on your Emeril Lagasse Air Fryer 360.

3. Rotate the temperature knob to 425°F and the timer for 25 minutes. Press the start button.

4. Allow the chicken to cook for 15 minutes, then flip and cook for the remaining minutes.

5. Let rest before serving.

Rotisserie Chicken

Preparation time
60 MINUTES

Cooking time
55 MINUTES

Servings
8

Ratings

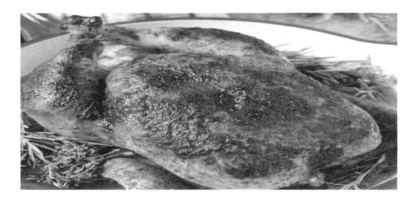

Ingredients

1/4 cup Rustic rub

4 lb. whole chicken

Nutritional Info

Calories: 282kcal

Carbs: 0g

Fat: 14g,

Protein: 44g

Directions

1. Rub the chicken with the rustic rub.

2. Fix the rotisserie spit on one side then slide the chicken so the split can run through the chicken. fix the fork and screws.

3. Select the rotisserie setting in the Emeril Lagasse Air Fryer 360. Set the temperature at 350°F for 55 minutes. Press the start button.

4. The chicken should have an internal temperature of 160°F when the cooking cycle is complete. Otherwise, add more minutes.

5. Let the chicken rest for 15 minutes before serving.

Turkey Meatloaf

Preparation time
1 HOUR 15 MINUTES

Cooking time
50 MINUTES

Servings
6

Ratings

Ingredients

1-1/2 lb. ground turkey
2/3 cup yellow onion, chopped
1/2 cup green bell pepper, chopped
1/2 cup dry breadcrumbs, unseasoned
1/3 cup celery, chopped
1 egg, beaten
1/2 cup ketchup
1 tbsp. garlic, minced
1 tbsp. Emeril original Essence
1/2 tbsp. salt
1/2 tbsp. black pepper, ground
1 tbsp. hot sauce

Nutritional Info

Calories: 193kcal
Carbs: 15g
Fat: 8g,
Protein: 15g

Directions

1. Place turkey in a mixing bowl. Add yellow onion, green bell pepper, breadcrumbs, celery, egg, 1 tablespoon ketchup, garlic, essence, salt, and black pepper.

2. Mix until well combined. Fill a loaf pan halfway with the batter and form it into a dome.

3. Add the remaining ketchup to a small mixing bowl and add the hot sauce. Spoon the mixture on the meatloaf then spread it using the back of the spoon.

4. Place the loaf pan on the pizza rack of the Emeril Lagasse Air Fryer 360 and select bake. Set the temperature at 375°F for 50 minutes. Press start.

5. The meatloaf should have turned golden brown and have an internal temperature of 165°F.

6. Let rest for 5 minutes before serving. Enjoy.

Pecan Crusted Chicken

 Preparation time
22 MINUTES

 Cooking time
15 MINUTES

Servings
6

Ratings

Ingredients

1 cup pecan pieces

1/2 cup breadcrumbs

3 tbsp. Creole seasoning

2 eggs

1/ cup olive oil

2 lb. chicken breast, skinless and boneless

1/2 cup mayonnaise

2 tbsp. honey

2 tbsp. Creole mustard

1 pinch salt

1 pinch cayenne pepper, ground

Nutritional Info

Calories: 259kcal

Carbs: 16g

Fat: 10g,

Protein: 25g

Directions

1. Combine pecans, breadcrumbs, and 2 tbsp. Creole seasoning in a food processor. Pulse for a minute to mix. Pour the mixture on a dish.

2. Beat eggs in a mixing bowl, then add oil and the remaining Creole.

3. Dip the chicken breast in the egg mixture, then in the pecan mixture shaking to remove excess.

4. Place the chicken on a baking pan. Place the crisper tray on the pizza rack and place the baking pan on top of both.

5. Select air fry setting on Emeril Lagasse Air Fryer 360 and Set temperature at 360°F for 15 minutes. Press start.

6. Meanwhile, mix honey, mustard, salt, and pepper until well combined.

7. During the cooking cycle, season the chicken breast with salt and pepper. Serve with the sauce and enjoy it.

Vegetables
and Side
Dishes

Flavorful Potato Casserole

Preparation time
10 MINUTES

Cooking time
30 MINUTES

Servings
6

Ratings

Ingredients

2 lb potatoes, peel & shredded

1 1/2 cups sour cream

2 cups cheddar cheese, shredded

1/4 cup parsley, chopped

1/4 cup dill, chopped

1 small onion, minced

Pepper

Salt

Nutritional Info

Calories 328

Fat: 24.7 g

Carbohydrates: 15.5 g

Sugar: 1.2 g

Protein: 13 g

Cholesterol: 65 mg

Directions

1. Prepare a 9x13-inch baking pan by spraying it with cooking spray and setting it aside.

2. Add all ingredients into the mixing bowl and mix until well combined.

3. Pour mixture into the prepared baking pan.

4. Select bake mode. Set the temperature to 425 F and the timer for 30 minutes. Press start.

5. Let the air fryer preheat then insert the pizza rack into shelf position 5.

6. Place baking pan on the pizza rack and bake.

7. Serve and enjoy.

Butternut Squash Cubes

 Preparation time
10 MINUTES

 Cooking time
30 MINUTES

 Servings
6

Ratings

Ingredients

2 lbs butternut squash, peel & cut into 1/2-inch cubes

2 tsp thyme, chopped

2 garlic cloves, crushed

2 tbsp maple syrup

2 tbsp olive oil

1 tsp salt

Nutritional Info

Calories 128

Fat: 4.9 g

Carbohydrates: 22.7 g

Sugar: 7.3 g

Protein: 1.6 g

Cholesterol: 0 mg

Directions

1. In a small bowl, whisk oil, thyme, garlic, maple syrup, and salt.

2. Add butternut squash into the mixing bowl. Pour oil mixture over butternut squash and toss well.

3. Spread butternut squash on a baking sheet.

4. Select bake mode. Set the oven to 400°F and timer to 30 minutes. Press start.

5. Let the air fryer preheat then insert the pizza rack into shelf position 5.

6. Place baking sheet on the pizza rack and bake.

7. Serve and enjoy.

Cheesy Baked Cabbage

 Preparation time
10 MINUTES

 Cooking time
10 MINUTES

Servings
6

Ratings

Ingredients

2 medium cabbage heads, cored & cut into 2-inch pieces

2 tbsp white sugar

3 tbsp flour

4 tbsp butter, melted

1 1/2 cups milk

1/2 tbsp white pepper

3/4 cup Swiss cheese, shredded

3/4 cup American cheese, shredded

1 tbsp salt

Nutritional Info

Calories 303

Fat: 16.6 g

Carbohydrates: 29.7 g

Sugar: 17.7 g

Protein: 12.7 g

Cholesterol 49 mg

Directions

1. Steam the cabbage. In a mixing bowl, mix cabbage, sugar, flour, butter, milk, and salt.

2. Transfer cabbage mixture into the baking dish. Sprinkle cheese on top.

3. Select bake mode. Set the temperature to 350 F and the timer for 10 minutes. Press start.

4. Let the air fryer preheat then insert the pizza rack into shelf position 5.

5. Place baking dish on the pizza rack and bake.

6. Serve and enjoy.

Spinach Zucchini Casserole

 Preparation time
10 MINUTES

 Cooking time
40 MINUTES

 Servings
6

Ratings

Ingredients

2 egg whites
2 tsp garlic powder
1/2 tsp pepper
1/4 cup parmesan cheese, grated
2 small yellow squash, diced
1/2 cup breadcrumbs
1 tsp dried basil
2 small zucchini, diced
1/4 cup feta cheese, crumbled
3 cups baby spinach
1 tbsp olive oil
1/2 tsp kosher salt

Nutritional Info

Calories 109
Fat: 5.2 g
Carbohydrates: 10.9 g
Sugar: 2.6 g
Protein: 6.1 g
Cholesterol: 8 mg

Directions

1. Prepare a 9x13-inch casserole dish by spraying it with cooking spray and setting it aside.

2. In a medium-sized skillet, heat the oil.

3. Add zucchini, yellow squash, and spinach and cook until spinach is wilted about 5 minutes.

4. Transfer zucchini mixture into the mixing bowl. Add remaining ingredients and mix well.

5. Spread mixture into the prepared casserole dish.

6. Select bake mode. Set the oven to 400°F and timer to 30 minutes. Press start.

7. Let the air fryer preheat then insert the pizza rack into shelf position 5.

8. Place casserole dish on the pizza rack and bake.

9. Serve and enjoy.

Tomato Squash Zucchini Bake

Preparation time
10 MINUTES

Cooking time
30 MINUTES

Servings
6

Ratings

Ingredients

3 tomatoes, sliced

2 medium zucchinis, sliced

3/4 cup parmesan cheese, shredded

1 tbsp olive oil

2 yellow squash, sliced

Pepper

Salt

Nutritional Info

Calories 88

Fat: 5.1 g

Carbohydrates: 7.2 g

Sugar: 3.9 g

Protein: 5.7 g

Cholesterol: 8 mg

Directions

1. Prepare a 9x13-inch baking pan by spraying it with cooking spray and setting it aside.

2. Arrange sliced tomatoes, squash, and zucchinis alternately in the baking dish.

3. Drizzle with oil and season with pepper and salt.

4. Sprinkle parmesan cheese on top of vegetables.

5. Select bake mode. Set the temperature to 350 F and the timer for 30 minutes. Press start.

6. Let the air fryer preheat then insert the pizza rack into shelf position 5.

7. Place baking dish on the pizza rack and cook.

8. Serve and enjoy.

Baked Vegetables

Preparation time
10 MINUTES

Cooking time
35 MINUTES

Servings
4

Ratings

Ingredients

3 cups Brussels sprouts, cut in half

2 zucchini, cut in a thicknessof 1/2-inch half circles

2 bell peppers, cut into 2-inch chunks

1 tsp thyme

8 oz mushrooms, cut in half

1 onion, cut into wedges

2 tbsp vinegar

1/4 cup olive oil

1/2 tsp salt

Nutritional Info

Calories 197

Fat: 13.4 g

Carbohydrates: 18.4 g

Sugar: 8.3 g

Protein: 6.1 g

Cholesterol: 0 mg

Directions

1. Prepare a baking sheet by lining it with parchment paper and setting it aside.

2. Add vegetables into the zip-lock bag.

3. Mix thyme, vinegar, oil, and salt and pour over vegetables.

4. Seal zip-lock bag and shake well and place it in the refrigerator for 1 hour.

5. Spread marinated vegetables on a baking sheet.

6. Select bake mode. Set the temperature knob to 375 F and the timer for 35 minutes. Press start.

7. Let the air fryer preheat then insert the pizza rack into shelf position 5.

8. Place baking sheet on the pizza rack and cook.

9. Serve and enjoy.

Cheesy Brussels Sprouts

 Preparation time
10 MINUTES

 Cooking time
25 MINUTES

 Servings
4

Ratings

★ ★ ★
★

Ingredients

15 oz Brussels sprouts, trimmed
and cut in half

1/4 cup parmesan cheese,
grated

3 garlic cloves, minced

1/4 cup breadcrumbs

3 tbsp olive oil

Pepper

Salt

Nutritional Info

Calories 184

Fat: 12.4 g

Carbohydrates: 15.5 g

Sugar: 2.7 g

Protein: 6.5 g

Cholesterol: 4 mg

Directions

1. Line baking sheet with parchment paper and set aside.

2. In a bowl, toss Brussels sprouts with breadcrumbs, cheese, garlic, oil, pepper, and salt until well coated.

3. Arrange Brussels sprouts on a baking sheet.

4. Select bake mode. Set the temperature knob to 390 F and the timer for 25 minutes. Press start.

5. Let the air fryer preheat then insert the pizza rack into shelf position 5.

6. Place baking sheet on the pizza rack and cook.

7. Serve and enjoy.

Healthy Zucchini Bake

Preparation time
10 MINUTES

Cooking time
45 MINUTES

Servings
6

Ratings

Ingredients

3 zucchini, grated

1/2 cup mozzarella cheese, shredded

1/2 cup feta cheese, crumbled

1/2 cup dill, chopped

3 eggs, lightly beaten

3 tbsp butter, melted

1/2 cup flour

Pepper

Salt

Nutritional Info

Calories 186

Fat: 11.5 g

Carbohydrates: 14.2 g

Sugar: 2.4 g

Protein: 8.4 g

Cholesterol: 109 mg

Directions

1. Prepare a 9-inch baking pan by spraying with cooking spray and set aside.

2. In a bowl, mix together zucchini, cheeses, dill, eggs, butter, pepper, flour, and salt.

3. Pour the zucchini mixture into the baking dish.

4. Select bake mode. Set the temperature to 350 F and the timer for 45 minutes. Press start.

5. Let the air fryer preheat then insert the pizza rack into shelf position 5.

6. Place baking dish on the pizza rack and cook.

7. Serve and enjoy.

Green Bean Casserole

Preparation time
10 MINUTES

Cooking time
25 MINUTES

Servings
4

Ratings

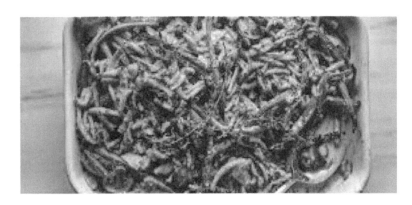

Ingredients

1 lb green beans, cut into pieces and trimmed

1/4 cup parmesan cheese, shredded

1/4 cup olive oil

2 oz pecans, crushed

1 small onion, chopped

2 tbsp lemon zest

Nutritional Info

Calories 269

Fat: 24.1 g

Carbohydrates: 12.6 g

Sugar: 3 g

Protein: 5.7 g

Cholesterol: 4 mg

Directions

1. Add all ingredients into the bowl and toss well.

2. Spread green bean mixture into the baking dish.

3. Select bake mode. Set the temperature knob to 390 F and the timer for 25 minutes. Press start.

4. Let the air fryer preheat then insert the pizza rack into shelf position 5.

5. Place baking dish on the pizza rack and cook.

6. Serve and enjoy.

Eggplant Zucchini Casserole

 Preparation time
10 MINUTES

 Cooking time
35 MINUTES

 Servings
6

Ratings

Ingredients

3 zucchini, sliced

4 tbsp basil, chopped

3 oz parmesan cheese, grated

1/4 cup parsley, chopped

1 cup cherry tomatoes, halved

1 medium eggplant, sliced

1 tbsp olive oil

3 garlic cloves, minced

1/4 tsp pepper

1/4 tsp salt

Nutritional Info

Calories 109

Fat: 5.8 g

Carbohydrates: 10.2 g

Sugar: 4.8 g

Protein: 7 g

Cholesterol: 10 mg

Directions

1. Prepare a baking pan by spraying with cooking spray and set aside.

2. Mix thoroughly all of the ingredients together in a big mixing bowl.

3. Pour eggplant mixture into the baking dish.

4. Select bake mode. Set the temperature to 350 F and the timer for 35 minutes. Press start.

5. Let the air fryer preheat then insert the pizza rack into shelf position 5.

6. Place baking dish on the pizza rack and cook.

7. Serve and enjoy.

Air Fryer Brussels Sprouts

Preparation time
10 MINUTES

Cooking time
14 MINUTES

Servings
2

Ratings

Ingredients

1/2 lb Brussels sprouts, halved and trimmed

Salt

1/2 tsp chili powder

Pepper

1/2 tbsp olive oil

1 tbsp chives, chopped

1/4 tsp cayenne

Nutritional Info

Calories 82

Fat: 4.1 g

Carbohydrates: 10.9 g

Sugar: 2.6 g

Protein: 4 g

Cholesterol: 0 mg

Directions

1. In a big container add all ingredients and toss well.

2. Spread Brussels sprouts in a crispier tray.

3. Place the drip tray below the bottom of the air fryer.

4. Insert the crispier tray into shelf position 4.

5. Select air fry mode. Set the temperature to 370 F and the timer for 14 minutes. Press start.

6. Serve and enjoy.

Rosemary Garlic Potatoes

Preparation time
10 MINUTES

Cooking time
15 MINUTES

Servings
4

Ratings

Ingredients

4 cups baby potatoes, cut into four pieces each

2 tsp dried rosemary, minced

3 tbsp olive oil

1/4 cup fresh parsley, chopped

1 tbsp garlic, minced

1 tbsp fresh lemon juice

Pepper

Salt

Nutritional Info

Calories 148

Fat: 10.8 g

Carbohydrates: 12.3 g

Sugar: 0.1 g

Protein: 2.6 g

Cholesterol: 0 mg

Directions

1. In a large bowl, add potatoes, garlic, rosemary, oil, pepper, and salt and toss well.

2. Spread potatoes in a crispier tray.

3. Place the drip tray below the bottom of the air fryer.

4. Insert the crispier tray into shelf position 4.

5. Select air fry mode. Set the temperature knob to 400 F and the timer for 15 minutes. Press start.

6. Transfer roasted potatoes in a bowl and toss with parsley and lemon juice.

7. Serve and enjoy.

Stuffed Peppers

Preparation time
10 MINUTES

Cooking time
25 MINUTES

Servings
6

Ratings

Ingredients

3 bell peppers, cut in half & remove seeds

1/4 cup feta cheese, crumbled

1/2 cup grape tomatoes, sliced

1/3 cup chickpeas, rinsed

1/2 tsp oregano

2 garlic cloves, minced

1 1/2 cups cooked quinoa

1/2 tsp salt

Nutritional Info

Calories 237

Fat: 4.8 g

Carbohydrates: 39.8 g

Sugar: 4.9 g

Protein: 9.8 g

Cholesterol: 6 mg

Directions

1. In a bowl, mix cooked quinoa, tomatoes, chickpeas, oregano, garlic, and salt.

2. Stuff quinoa mixture into the bell pepper halves and place in a baking dish.

3. Select bake mode. Set the temperature knob to 400 F and the timer for 25 minutes. Press start.

4. Let the air fryer preheat then insert the pizza rack into shelf position 5.

5. Place baking dish on the pizza rack and cook.

6. Top peppers with crumbled cheese and serve.

Air Fryer Garlic Mushrooms

Preparation time
10 MINUTES

Cooking time
15 MINUTES

Servings
4

Ratings

Ingredients

15 oz baby portobello mushrooms, halved

2 tbsp butter, melted

2 tsp coconut aminos

2 tsp garlic, minced

Nutritional Info

Calories 321

Fat: 5.8 g

Carbohydrates: 40.8 g

Sugar: 0 g

Protein: 40 g

Cholesterol: 15 mg

Directions

1. In a bowl, toss mushrooms with coconut aminos, garlic, and butter.

2. Add mushrooms to the crispier tray.

3. Place the drip tray below the bottom of the air fryer.

4. Insert the crispier tray into shelf position 4.

5. Select air fry mode. Set the temperature knob to 400 F and the timer for 15 minutes. Press start.

6. Serve and enjoy.

Lemon Cheese Asparagus

Preparation time
10 MINUTES

Cooking time
10 MINUTES

Servings
4

Ratings

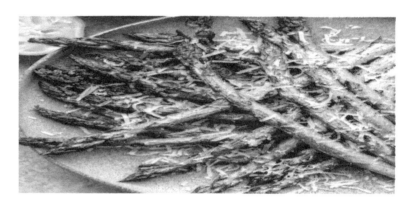

Ingredients

1 lb asparagus, cut woody ends and trimmed

1 tbsp fresh lemon juice

1 tsp olive oil

1 oz feta cheese, crumbled

Pepper

Salt

Nutritional Info

Calories 52

Fat: 2.9 g

Carbohydrates: 4.8 g

Sugar: 2.5 g

Protein: 3.5 g

Cholesterol: 6 mg

Directions

1. Toss asparagus with lemon juice, olive oil, pepper, and salt in a bowl.

2. Add asparagus to a crispier tray.

3. Place the drip tray below the bottom of the air fryer.

4. Insert the crispier tray into shelf position 4.

5. Select air fry mode. Set the temperature knob to 400 F and the timer for 10 minutes. Press start.

6. Top with feta cheese and serve.

Tasty Green Beans with Onion

 Preparation time
10 MINUTES

 Cooking time
6 MINUTES

 Servings
4

Ratings

Ingredients

1 lb green beans, trimmed

1/2 cup onion, sliced

2 tbsp olive oil

Pepper

Salt

Nutritional Info

Calories 101

Fat: 7.2 g

Carbohydrates: 9.5 g

Sugar: 2.2 g

Protein: 2.2 g

Cholesterol: 0 mg

Directions

1. In a bowl, toss green beans with oil, sliced onion, pepper, and salt.

2. Add green beans and onion to the crispier tray.

3. Place the drip tray below the bottom of the air fryer.

4. Insert the crispier tray into shelf position 4.

5. Select air fry mode. Set the temperature knob to 330 F and the timer for 6 minutes. Press start.

6. Serve and enjoy.

Curried Cauliflower Florets

Preparation time
10 MINUTES

Cooking time
10 MINUTES

Servings
4

Ratings

Ingredients

1 small cauliflower head, cut into florets

1 tbsp curry powder

2 tbsp olive oil

1/4 tsp salt

Nutritional Info

Calories 82

Fat: 7.3 g

Carbohydrates: 4.4 g

Sugar: 1.6 g

Protein: 1.5 g

Cholesterol: 0 mg

Directions

1. In a bowl, toss cauliflower florets with oil, curry powder, and salt.

2. Add cauliflower florets in a crispier tray.

3. Place the drip tray below the bottom of the air fryer.

4. Insert the crispier tray into shelf position 4.

5. Select air fry mode. Set the temperature knob to 350 F and the timer for 10 minutes. Press start.

6. Serve and enjoy.

Flavorful Cauliflower Florets

 Preparation time
10 MINUTES

 Cooking time
20 MINUTES

 Servings
4

Ratings

Ingredients

5 cups cauliflower florets
6 garlic cloves, chopped
4 tablespoons olive oil
1/2 tsp cumin powder
1/2 tsp ground coriander
1/2 tsp salt

Nutritional Info

Calories 159
Fat: 14.2 g
Carbohydrates: 8.2 g
Sugar: 3.1 g
Protein: 2.8 g
Cholesterol: 0 mg

Directions

1. Add cauliflower florets and remaining ingredients into the large bowl and toss well.

2. Add cauliflower florets in a crispier tray.

3. Place the drip tray below the bottom of the air fryer.

4. Insert the crispier tray into shelf position 4.

5. Select air fry mode. Set the temperature knob to 400 F and the timer for 20 minutes. Press start.

6. Stir cauliflower florets halfway through.

7. Serve and enjoy.

Crispy Eggplant

Preparation time
10 MINUTES

Cooking time
20 MINUTES

Servings
4

Ratings

Ingredients

1 eggplant, cut into 1-inch pieces
1/2 tsp red pepper
1 tsp garlic powder
2 tbsp olive oil
1/2 tsp Italian seasoning
1 tsp paprika

Nutritional Info

Calories 99
Fat: 7.5 g
Carbohydrates: 8.7 g
Sugar: 4.5 g
Protein: 1.5 g
Cholesterol: 0 mg

Directions

1. Add eggplant and remaining ingredients into the bowl and toss well.

2. Add eggplant to the crispier tray.

3. Place the drip tray below the bottom of the air fryer.

4. Insert the crispier tray into shelf position 4.

5. Select air fry mode. Set the temperature knob to 375 F and the timer for 20 minutes. Press start.

6. Stir eggplant pieces halfway through.

7. Serve and enjoy.

Appetizer

Mozzarella Stuffed Mushrooms

Preparation time
10 MINUTES

Cooking time
10 MINUTES

Servings
12

Ratings

Ingredients

1 cup tomato sauce

2 teaspoons fresh basil, chopped

12 large mushroom caps

1 cup mozzarella cheese, shredded

Nutritional Info

Calories: 112kcal

Carbs: 7.5g

Fat: 5.4g,

Protein: 10.5g

Directions

1. Mix the tomato sauce and basil leaves in a bowl.

2. Stuff the mushrooms with the mixture.

3. Sprinkle cheese on top.

4. Arrange mushroom caps inside the air fryer oven.

5. Select roast function.

6. Cook at 380 degrees F for 7 minutes.

Serving suggestion

Garnish with sliced basil leaves.

Tip

Do not rinse mushrooms. Instead, clean with a damp paper towel.

Tortilla Chips with Salsa

 Preparation time
10 MINUTES

 Cooking time
10 MINUTES

 Servings
6

Ratings

Ingredients

10 tortillas
Cooking spray
Salt to taste
3 cups salsa

Nutritional Info

Calories: 338kcal
Carbs: 43g
Fat: 17.0g,
Protein: 5g

Directions

1. Spray both sides of tortillas with oil.

2. Sprinkle with salt.

3. Slice into wedges.

4. Place the wedges in the air crisper tray.

5. Choose air fry option.

6. Cook at 350 degrees F for 4 minutes.

7. Flip and cook for another 3 minutes.

8. Serve with salsa.

Serving suggestion

Sprinkle with a little salt before serving.

Tip

Drain on a plate lined with paper towels.

Baked Ricotta with Herbs

 Preparation time
10 MINUTES

 Cooking time
10 MINUTES

 Servings
8 TO 10

Ratings

Ingredients

30 oz. ricotta

4 teaspoons rosemary, chopped

4 eggs, beaten

1 tablespoon lemon zest

6 tablespoons Parmesan cheese

Salt and pepper to taste

Nutritional Info

Calories: 177.2kcal

Carbs: 5.8g

Fat: 10.1g,

Protein: 15.1g

Directions

1. Combine all the ingredients in a bowl.

2. Spread mixture into a small baking pan.

3. Set the air fryer oven to air fry.

4. For 10 minutes cook at 380 degrees F.

Serving suggestion

Sprinkle with a little pepper before serving.

Tip

Stop cooking when the edges turn brown.

Roasted Goat Cheese and Tomato Tarts

 Preparation time
15 MINUTES

 Cooking time
5 MINUTES

 Servings
8

Ratings

Ingredients

1 tablespoon honey

1 teaspoon dried Italian seasoning

1/2 cup goat cheese, crumbled

1 pack crescent rounds, sliced into 8 rounds

2 tomatoes, sliced

2 tablespoons olive oil

Nutritional Info

Calories: 198.4kcal

Carbs: 16.2g

Fat: 12.6g,

Protein: 4.3g

Directions

1. In a bowl, mix honey, Italian seasoning and goat cheese.

2. Press the dough to form a flat circle.

3. Top the dough rounds with the honey mixture.

4. Put tomato slices on top.

5. Drizzle with olive oil.

6. Place these inside the air fryer oven.

7. Set the air fryer oven to roast.

8. For 5 minutes cook at 350 degrees F.

Serving suggestion

Sprinkle with pepper.

Tip

You can also use cream cheese for this recipe.

Chicken Nachos

Preparation time
15 MINUTES

Cooking time
5 MINUTES

Servings
4

Ratings

Ingredients

2 cups tortilla chips

1/2 cup chicken, cooked and shredded

1/2 cup black beans, rinsed and drained

1 jalapeno, sliced

1/2 cup fresh cheese, grated

1/2 cup cheddar cheese, shredded

Directions

1. Spread the tortillas chips in a baking pan.

2. Sprinkle the chicken, beans, jalapeno and cheeses on top.

3. Set the pan inside the air fryer oven.

4. Choose bake setting.

5. Cook at 350 degrees F for 3 to 5 minutes or until cheese has melted.

Nutritional Info

Calories: 399.3kcal

Carbs: 12.9g

Fat: 11.2g,

Protein: 59.1g

Serving suggestion

Serve with guacamole, lime wedges, sour cream and salsa.

Tip

You can also top nachos with chopped tomatoes.

Baked Potato Rounds

Preparation time
10 MINUTES

Cooking time
20 MINUTES

Servings
8

Ratings

Ingredients

2 potatoes, sliced into ½ inch thick rounds

Cooking spray

Salt and pepper to taste

1 cup sour cream

1 cup cheddar cheese, shredded

Nutritional Info

Calories: 160kcal

Carbs: 21g

Fat: 8g,

Protein: 2g

Directions

1. Spray potato rounds with oil.
2. Sprinkle with salt and pepper.
3. Add the potato rounds to the air crisper tray.
4. Select air fry setting.
5. Cook at 370 degrees F for 15 minutes, flipping once.
6. Let cool.
7. Top with sour cream and cheddar cheese.
8. Put these back to the air fryer oven.
9. Choose bake setting.
10. Bake at 350 degrees F for 3 minutes or until cheese has melted.

Serving suggestion

Sprinkle with dried herbs.

Tip

Use Russet potatoes for this recipe.

Bacon Wrapped Asparagus

Preparation time
5 MINUTES

Cooking time
10 MINUTES

Servings
8

Ratings

Ingredients

1 lb. asparagus, trimmed

6 slices bacon

Nutritional Info

Calories: 109.6kcal

Carbs: 3.7g

Fat: 8g,

Protcin: 6.6g

Directions

1. Wrap a couple of asparagus with bacon slices.

2. Organize in an air crisper tray in a single layer.

3. Set your air fryer oven to air fry.

4. For 10 minutes cook at 380 degrees F.

Tip

Before air frying, you can also sprinkle with maple syrup.STOP

Italian Olives

Preparation time
10 MINUTES

Cooking time
5 MINUTES

Servings
8

Ratings

Ingredients

2 cups green olives, pitted

2 cups black olives, pitted

2 tablespoons olive oil

2 cloves garlic, minced

½ teaspoon dried fennel seeds

½ teaspoon dried oregano

Pinch red pepper flakes

Salt and pepper to taste

Nutritional Info

Calories: 113kcal

Carbs: 0g

Fat: 0g,

Protein: 13g

Directions

1. Toss all the ingredients in a bowl.

2. Mix well.

3. Spread the olives in the air crisper tray.

4. Choose air fry setting.

5. Set temperature to 300 degrees F.

6. Cook for 5 minutes.

Serving suggestion

Serve immediately.

Tip

You can also use garlic powder instead of minced garlic.

Mini Lemon Crab Cakes

Preparation time
45 MINUTES

Cooking time
MINUTES

Servings
12

Ratings

Ingredients

24 oz. crab meat

3 green onions, chopped

3 tablespoons lemon juice

3 teaspoons lemon zest

6 tablespoons breadcrumbs

6 tablespoons mayonnaise

Nutritional Info

Calories: 24kcal

Carbs: 3g

Fat: 0g,

Protein: 2g

Directions

1. Combine all the ingredients in a bowl.

2. Shape into 24 small patties.

3. Refrigerate for 30 minutes.

4. Add the mini crab cakes to the air crisper tray.

5. Set your air fryer oven to air fry.

6. Cook at 370 degrees F for 5 minutes per side or until golden and crispy.

Serving suggestion

Garnish with half lemon slices.

Tip

You can also add fish flakes to the mixture.

Bacon Wrapped Dates

 Preparation time
5 MINUTES

 Cooking time
10 MINUTES

 Servings
12

Ratings

Ingredients

12 slices bacon

24 dates, pitted

Nutritional Info

Calories: 49.6kcal

Carbs: 6.3g

Fat: 2.3g,

Protein: 1.6g

Directions

1. Slice the bacon in half.

2. Wrap each date with a bacon slice.

3. Organize in a single layer in the air crisper tray.

4. Choose air fry setting.

5. Cook at 400 degrees F for 7 to 8 minutes.

Serving suggestion

Insert toothpick before serving.

Tip

You can also dip in balsamic vinegar before air frying.

Pizza Chips

 Preparation time
15 MINUTES

 Cooking time
MINUTES

 Servings
12

Ratings

Ingredients

12 cheddar cheese slices, sliced into 4 smaller pieces

12 pepperoni slices, chopped

2 tablespoons dried oregano

Nutritional Info

Calories: 160kcal

Carbs: 14g

Fat: 10g,

Protein: 2g

Directions

1. Top the cheese slices with pepperoni and oregano.

2. Place these in the air crisper tray.

3. Choose air fry setting in your air fryer oven.

4. For 5 minutes cook at 350 degrees F.

Serving suggestion

Let cool to harden before serving.

Tip

You can also use a cracker and top it with the cheese.

Mini Clam Patties

 Preparation time
10 MINUTES

 Cooking time
5 MINUTES

 Servings
8

Ratings

Ingredients

2 lb. clam meat, chopped
1 onion, minced
1 teaspoon garlic powder
2 stalks green onion, chopped
1/4 cup breadcrumbs
1 egg, beaten
Cooking spray

Nutritional Info

Calories: 1260kcal
Carbs: 112.6g
Fat: 55.6g,
Protein: 72.9g

Directions

1. Combine all the ingredients in a bowl.

2. Shape into 16 small patties.

3. Spray with oil.

4. Transfer patties to the air crisper tray.

5. Set your air fryer oven to air fry.

6. For 5 minutes cook at 350 degrees F per side or until golden and crispy.

Serving suggestion

Serve with sweet chili sauce.

Tip

You can also add fish flakes to the mixture.

Cheese Chips

 Preparation time
10 MINUTES

 Cooking time
5 MINUTES

 Servings
12

Ratings

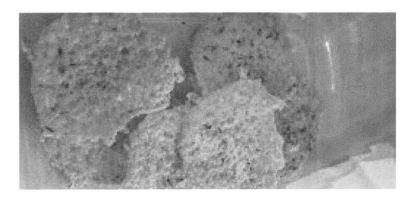

Ingredients

12 cheddar slices, sliced into 4 pieces
Cooking spray

Nutritional Info

Calories: 456kcal
Carbs: 3.7g
Fat: 30g,
Protein: 41.6g

Directions

1. Spray cheese slices with oil.
2. Organize in a single layer in the air crisper tray.
3. Choose air fry setting.
4. For 5 minutes cook at 350 degrees F, turning once.

Serving suggestion

Sprinkle with dried Italian herbs.

Tip

You can Keep for up to 3 days in an airtight jar.

Mushrooms with Bacon and Cheese

 Preparation time
15 MINUTES

 Cooking time
MINUTES

 Servings
12

Ratings

Ingredients

3 tablespoons butter, melted

8 oz. cream cheese

8 strips bacon, cooked and chopped

Salt and pepper to taste

24 mushrooms

Nutritional Info

Calories: 14.5kcal

Carbs: 0.6g

Fat: 0.5g,

Protein: 1.7g.

Directions

1. Combine butter, cream cheese, bacon, salt and pepper in a bowl.

2. Top mushrooms with the mixture.

3. Place the mushrooms inside the air fryer oven.

4. Set the air fryer oven to roast.

5. for 5 minutes cook at 350 degrees F.

Serving suggestion

Garnish with chopped chives.

Tip

Use baby bell mushrooms or button mushrooms for this recipe.

Cranberry Brie Bites

Preparation time
10 MINUTES

Cooking time
7 MINUTES

Servings
12

Ratings

Ingredients

24 wonton wrappers

8 oz. brie cheese

2 cups cranberry sauce

Nutritional Info

Calories: 47.7kcal

Carbs: 8.5g

Fat: 1.5g,

Protein: 0.2g.

Directions

1. Line your muffin pan with wonton wrappers.

2. Place the muffin pan inside the air fryer oven.

3. Choose air fry setting.

4. For 3 minutes cook at 300 degrees F.

5. Top the wonton cups with cheese.

6. Place it back to the oven.

7. Select bake function.

8. Bake for 3 minutes or until cheese has melted.

9. Top with cranberry sauce and serve.

Serving suggestion

Garnish with cranberry slices.

Tip

You can also use other melty cheese.

Bacon Wrapped Cracker

 Preparation time
5 MINUTES

 Cooking time
5 MINUTES

 Servings
12

Ratings

Ingredients

12 crackers

12 slices bacon

1/4 cup Parmesan cheese, grated

Nutritional Info

Calories: 190kcal

Carbs: 23g

Fat: 9g,

Protein: 3g.

Directions

1. Wrap crackers with bacon slices.

2. Sprinkle with Parmesan cheese.

3. Place in the air crisper tray.

4. Choose air fry setting.

5. For 5 minutes cook at 350 degrees F per side or until bacon is crispy.

Serving suggestion

Serve with sweet chili sauce.

Tip

Do not overcrowd the air crisper tray.

Bruschetta

Preparation time
15 MINUTES

Cooking time
5 MINUTES

Servings
12

Ratings

Ingredients

4 tomatoes, chopped
1/4 cup fresh basil leaves, diced
1/4 cup Parmesan cheese, shredded
1 clove garlic, minced
1 tablespoon balsamic vinegar
1 teaspoon olive oil
Salt and pepper to taste
1 loaf French bread, sliced
Cooking spray

Nutritional Info

Calories: 67.1kcal
Carbs: 4.9g
Fat: 5.5g,
Protein: 0.7g.

Directions

1. In a bowl, incorporate all the ingredients except French bread.

2. Top the bread slices with the mixture.

3. Spray the bread with oil.

4. Organize in a single layer in the air crisper tray.

5. Choose toast or air fry setting.

6. For 2 to 3 minutes cook at 250 degrees F.

Serving suggestion

Sprinkle with pepper.

Tip

You can also use Italian bread for this recipe.

Pita Chips

 Preparation time
6 MINUTES

 Cooking time
4 MINUTES

 Servings
8

 Ratings

Ingredients

6 pita breads
4 tablespoons olive oil
2 teaspoons dried oregano
Pinch salt

Nutritional Info

Calories: 140kcal
Carbs: 18g
Fat: 6g,
Protein: 3g.

Directions

1. Slice pita bread into wedges.
2. Brush each side with olive oil.
3. Sprinkle with oregano and salt.
4. Organize in a single layer in the air crisper tray.
5. Set your air fryer oven to air fry.
6. Cook at 350 degrees F for 1 to 2 minutes per side.

Serving suggestion

Serve with ranch dip or French onion dip.

Tip

You can also season pita chips with Italian herbs.

Cakes, Cookies and Muffins

Banana Bundt Cake with Cream Cheese Icing

 Preparation time
25 MINUTES

 Cooking time
14 MINUTES

 Servings
8

Ratings

Ingredients

1 cup all-purpose flour

1 teaspoon baking powder

2 teaspoons vanilla extract

1/3 cup vegetable oil

1 egg

1/2 teaspoon cinnamon

1/2 teaspoon baking soda

2 bananas, peeled

2 oz. cream cheese, softened

2 tablespoons heavy cream

2 tablespoons butter, softened

3/4 cup sugar

1 cup powdered sugar

1/2 teaspoon salt

Nutritional Info

Calories: 407.8kcal

Carbs: 49.3g

Fat: 11.3g,

Protein: 9.3g.

Directions

1. In a small mixing bowl, crush the bananas and then add the egg.
2. Next add the oil, sugar, and 1 teaspoon vanilla extract. Mix well.
3. Gently sift the flour, baking soda, and cinnamon into the bowl with the banana.
4. Pour the mixture into a Bundt pan.
5. Choose the bake function in your air fryer oven.
6. Bake for 14 minutes at 32o°F.
7. Rotate the pan and continue baking for 16 minutes.
8. Let rest for 10 minutes.
9. Put butter and cream cheese in a microwavable bowl.
10. Microwave for 8 seconds until butter is melted.
11. Stir and cook for another 8 seconds.
12. Add powdered sugar and the remaining 1 teaspoon vanilla extract.
13. Add cream and whisk until you get your preferred consistency. More cream creates a thicker consistency.

Serving suggestion
Drizzle some cream cheese icing before serving.

Tip
If the top of the cake seems to be cooking faster or is turning brown quickly, place a sheet of foil on top.

Luscious Triple Berry Cobbler

 Preparation time
10 MINUTES

 Cooking time
12 MINUTES

 Servings
6

Ratings

Ingredients

3 tablespoons melted butter

1/4 cup flour

1/2 cup quick oats

1/2 cup raspberries or blackberries

1/2 cup strawberries

1 cup blueberries

2-1/8 cups of white sugar, divided

1 teaspoon lemon juice

1/4 cup brown sugar

1 teaspoon vanilla

Nutritional Info

Calories: 196kcal

Carbs: 35g

Fat: 5g,

Protein: 2.9g.

Directions

1. Combine berries, 1/8 cup white sugar, and lemon juice in a large mixing bowl.
2. In a separate bowl, mix flour, vanilla, oats, melted butter, brown sugar, and the other 1/8 cup of white sugar.
3. Mix well.
4. Coat pan with non-stick cooking spray.
5. Put the oats mixture in first.
6. Then add the berries.
7. Choose the bake function in your air fryer oven.
8. Bake for 12 minutes at 390°F.

Serving suggestion

Before serving, permit the cake to cool for ten minutes. Can be served with vanilla ice cream or whipped cream.

Tip

Garnish with fresh berries and mint leaves.

Chocolate Raspberry Lava Cake

Preparation time
5 MINUTES

Cooking time
10 MINUTES

Servings
3

Ratings

Ingredients

1 large egg

3 tablespoons all-purpose flour

3 tablespoons white sugar

6 tablespoons unsalted butter

1 large egg yolk

A pinch of salt

1/2 teaspoon vanilla extract

4 oz. semi-sweet chocolate bar, broke into smaller pieces

Fresh raspberries

Nutritional Info

Calories: 375kcal

Carbs: 38g

Fat: 26g,

Protein: 2.2g.

Directions

1. In a bowl that is microwave-safe, combine the butter and chocolate.

2. For 1 minute microwave, stirring every few seconds until melted. Set aside.

3. Grease 3 ramekins that are 6 oz. each. Set aside.

4. In a large bowl, combine the chocolate, flour, and salt. Mix well.

5. Fill each ramekin halfway.

6. Choose the air fry function.

7. Air fry for 8-10 minutes at 370°F.

Serving suggestion

Allow to cool for 1 minute before serving and sprinkle top with powdered sugar and add fresh raspberries.

Tip

You may also use whipped cream and vanilla ice cream as toppings.

Crumbly Air Fryer Carrot Cake

 Preparation time
50 MINUTES

 Cooking time
MINUTES

 Servings
6

Ratings

Ingredients

2/3 cup all-purpose flour
2 tablespoons dark brown sugar
1/2 cup buttermilk
1 teaspoon baking powder
1/4 teaspoon baking soda
3 tablespoons canola oil
2 teaspoons pumpkin pie spice
1/3 cup white whole wheat flour
1/3 cup walnuts, chopped and toasted
1/4 cup dried cranberries
1 large egg, lightly beaten
1 cup shredded carrots
1 teaspoon vanilla extract
1/3 cup white sugar plus another 2 more tablespoons
1/4 teaspoon salt
1 teaspoon orange zest, grated

Nutritional Info

Calories: 429kcal
Carbs: 5.6g
Fat: 40.2g,
Protein: 10.5g.

Directions

1. Preheat air fryer to 350°F.
2. Grease a 6-inch round baking pan and lightly dust with flour. Set aside.
3. Whisk together orange zest, buttermilk, vanilla, brown sugar, white sugar, oil, and egg in a large container.
4. In a separate container, combine flours, baking soda, salt, 1 teaspoon pumpkin spice, and baking powder.
5. Stir-in the egg mixture into the dry ingredients slowly.
6. Add dried cranberries and carrots.
7. Pour batter into baking pan.
8. Combine the remaining 2 tablespoons white sugar, 1 teaspoon pumpkin spice, and walnuts in a small bowl.
9. Sprinkle this mixture over the batter evenly.
10. Choose the air fry function in your air fryer oven.
11. Air fry for 35 minutes or until the toothpick comes out clean when checked.

Serving suggestion

Let the cake rest for 10 minutes and serve while still warm.

Tip

If the top appears to cook quicker than the rest of the cake, cover the top with foil.

Keto Friendly Chocolate Cake

Preparation time
5 MINUTES

Cooking time
10 MINUTES

Servings
6

Ratings

Ingredients

2 large eggs

1/3 cup unsweetened cocoa powder

1 teaspoon baking powder

1-1/2 cups almond flour

1/3 cup unsweetened almond milk

1 teaspoon vanilla extract

1/2 cup powdered swerve

1/4 teaspoon salt

Nutritional Info

Calories: 325kcal

Carbs: 37g

Fat: 14g,

Protein: 2.2g.

Directions

1. In a big mixing container, combine all of the ingredients.

2. Grease baking tin and pour in the batter.

3. Air fry for 10 minutes at 350°F.

Serving suggestion

Sprinkle powdered swerve before serving.

Tip

You can also chill the cake before serving.

Air Fryer Pandan Cake

Preparation time
10 MINUTES

Cooking time
25 MINUTES

Servings
2

Ratings

Ingredients

4-1/2 tablespoons plain flour

2 egg whites

2 egg yolks

1/4 tablespoon baking powder

2-1/3 tablespoon sugar

1 tablespoon coconut milk

1 teaspoon pandan essence or extract

1-1/3 teaspoon olive oil

Nutritional Info

Calories: 110kcal

Carbs: 16g

Fat: 4g,

Protein: 3g.

Directions

1. Sift the flour and baking powder in a bowl and set aside.
2. Preheat air fryer to 302°F.
3. Using a hand mixer, mix the egg white with half the sugar to make the meringue.
4. Add olive oil and mix.
5. Next add coconut milk, pandan essence, and flour.
6. Add 1/3 of the meringue to the flour mixture. Fold with a spatula.
7. Add the rest of the meringue and stir gently.
8. Pour mixture to a baking pan or tray.
9. Cover with foil and poke small holes on it with a toothpick.
10. Choose the air fry function in your air fryer oven.
11. Bake for 25 minutes.
12. Remove foil and bake for 5 more minutes.

Serving suggestion

Serve with whip cream or syrup.

Tip

Goes well with coffee or tea.

3 Ingredient Chocolate Mug Cake

 Preparation time
3 MINUTES

 Cooking time
13 MINUTES

 Servings
1

Ratings

Ingredients

1 tablespoon water

2 tablespoons unsweetened applesauce

6 tablespoons chocolate cake mix

Nutritional Info

Calories: 200kcal

Carbs: 28g

Fat: 6.7g,

Protein: 2.2g.

Directions

1. Whisk all ingredients until smooth.

2. Pour batter into an 8-oz. mug that can withstand high heat.

3. Choose the air fry function in your air fryer oven.

4. Air fry for 13 minutes or until cooked.

Serving suggestion

Let the mug cool first before serving. Top with chocolate syrup or frosting.

Tip

Be careful when taking out the mug.

Durian Burnt Cheesecake

Preparation time
23 MINUTES

Cooking time
MINUTES

Servings
4 OR MORE

Ratings

Ingredients

9 oz. chilled cream cheese
8 fl. cream
2 large eggs
5 tablespoons caster sugar
3-1/2 tablespoons cake flour
1 cup durian flesh

Nutritional Info

Calories: 143.5kcal
Carbs: 23.2g
Fat: 12.3g,
Protein: 3.5g.

Directions

1. Preheat air fryer to 392°F.

2. Line a 6-inch round baking tin.

3. Add all ingredients in a food processor until smooth.

4. Gently pour into a lined baking tin.

5. Choose bake function.

6. Bake for 23 minutes.

Serving suggestion

Let the cake cool for at least 20 minutes before serving. Garnish as desired.

Tip

Let some parchment paper protrude from the tin to make it easier to take out the cake.

Air Fryer Apple Cake

Preparation time
5 MINUTES

Cooking time
15 MINUTES

Servings
8

Ratings

Ingredients

1 cup all-purpose flours

3 eggs

1 cup brown sugar

1 cup apples, peeled and diced

Nutritional Info

Calories: 308kcal

Carbs: 43g

Fat: 15.9g,

Protein: 3.4g.

Directions

1. Combine eggs and sugar in a bowl until smooth.

2. Add flour and mix.

3. Add the apples making sure that all they are evenly coated with the batter.

4. Pour batter into a greased pan.

5. Choose the air fry function.

6. Air fry for 12-15 minutes at 320°F.

Serving suggestion

Sprinkle with powdered sugar and serve.

Tip

The duration of time it takes to cook depends on the thickness of the baking pan and the type of air fryer you're using. Use the toothpick method to check if the cake is cooked.

Toothsome Nutella Cake

 Preparation time
5 MINUTES

 Cooking time
13 MINUTES

 Servings
2

Ratings

Ingredients

1-1/2 cup Nutella
1/2 cup Nutella for frosting
4 eggs
1/2 cup all-purpose flour

Nutritional Info

Calories: 356kcal
Carbs: 33g
Fat: 18.7g,
Protein: 3.2g.

Directions

1. Mix Nutella, eggs, and flour in a large bowl until smooth.

2. Grease pan with oil or spray with non-stick oil.

3. Pour batter into pan.

4. Choose the air fry function.

5. Set temperature to°F.

6. Air fry for 13 minutes or until the center is fully cooked.

Serving suggestion

Let the cake cool for 10 minutes then apply the frosting.

Tip

Letting the cake cool will make it easier to remove from the pan.

Air Fryer Pumpkin Cake

 Preparation time
20 MINUTES

 Cooking time
MINUTES

 Servings
10

Ratings

Ingredients

1 tablespoon pumpkin pie spice
12 oz. evaporated milk
3 large room temperature eggs
1 cup walnuts, diced
1 package yellow cake mix
1 cup granulated sugar
15 oz. pumpkin puree
3/4 cup melted unsalted butter
8 tablespoons room temperature
butter for frosting
1 teaspoon ground cinnamon
8 oz. room temperature cream
cheese
1 cup powdered sugar
2 tablespoons vanilla extract

Nutritional Info

Calories: 223kcal
Carbs: 39.1g
Fat: 3.2g,
Protein: 9.6g.

Directions

1. Combine pumpkin puree, eggs, sugar, milk, ground cinnamon, and pumpkin spice in a large bowl.

2. Next add the cake mix, diced walnuts, and melted unsalted butter. Mix well.

3. Pour batter on greased pan or skillet.

4. Choose the bake function.

5. Bake for 15 minutes at 320°F.

6. In a separate bowl create frosting by combining cream cheese, butter, sugar, vanilla extract, and walnuts.

Serving suggestion

Let the cake cool down then apply the frosting. Garnish with more walnuts and a sprinkle of pumpkin spice on top.

Tip

Once the 15 minutes is up, stick a toothpick to check if the cake is done cooking. If not, add a few more minutes.

Mini Berry Cheese Cakes

Preparation time
20 MINUTES

Cooking time
15 MINUTES

Servings
8

Ratings

Ingredients

1/2 cup plus 2 teaspoons granulated sugar

1-1/2 cups graham cracker crumbs

8 oz. cream cheese, room temperature

1/4 cup melted butter

1/2 cup sour cream

8 oz. fresh blackberries

1 egg

1/2 teaspoon vanilla extract

1 teaspoon lemon juice

Nutritional Info

Calories: 59.1kcal

Carbs: 6.2g

Fat: 2.1g,

Protein: 1.7g.

Directions

1. Mix butter, sugar, and graham crumbs.
2. Scoop and push graham mixture to the bottom of each muffin liner.
3. In another container, combine cream cheese, sour cream, sugar, vanilla, egg, and lemon juice until smooth.
4. On top of the graham crumbs spread the cream cheese mixture, almost filling the muffin tin.
5. Choose the air fry function.
6. Air fry for 15 minutes at 320°F or until the center is set.
7. Let cakes cool and refrigerate for 3-4 hours.

Serving suggestion

Sprinkle with powdered sugar and garnish with fresh blackberries.

Tip

You can put one blackberry at the center of the cheesecake for a pleasant surprise.

Copycat Recipe Starbucks Coffee Cake

 Preparation time
20 MINUTES

 Cooking time
12 MINUTES

 Servings
6

Ratings

Ingredients

1 teaspoon ground cinnamon with 1 teaspoon for topping
1/3 cup half and half or light cream
1 cup room temperature butter plus ½ cup for topping
1 teaspoon salt
3/4 cup brown sugar plus 1 cup for topping
1/2 cup white sugar
1 teaspoon baking powder
2 eggs
2 cups flour plus 1 cup for topping
1 teaspoon vanilla
1/2 cup pecan, diced

Nutritional Info

Calories: 112.3kcal
Carbs: 27.9g
Fat: 12.3g,
Protein: 6.2g.

Directions

1. Combine 1 cup butter, ¾ cup brown sugar, and white sugar in a bowl until creamy.
2. Add baking powder, eggs, flour, vanilla, salt, and half & half. Mix well.
3. Coat pan with olive oil and pour the batter in.
4. In a separate bowl, combine 1 cup brown sugar, 1 cup flour, ½ cup butter, and 1 teaspoon cinnamon.
5. Fold in the pecans.
6. Spread the pecan mixture over the batter.
7. Choose the air fry function.
8. Set temperature for 320°F.
9. Air fry for 12 minutes or until the toothpick comes out clean.

Serving suggestion

Let the cake cool for a few minutes before serving.

Tip

You can leave out the salt if you are using salted butter.

Heavenly Chocolate Cherry Dump Cake

Preparation time
5 MINUTES

Cooking time
12 MINUTES

Servings
6

Ratings

Ingredients

1 package Devil's Food Cake mix

1 container chocolate frosting

2 large eggs

1/2 cup chocolate chips

1 teaspoon vanilla

21 oz. canned cherry

Nutritional Info

Calories: 375kcal

Carbs: 38g

Fat: 26g,

Protein: 2.2g.

Directions

1. Combine cherries, cake mix, eggs, chocolate chips, and vanilla in a large mixing bowl.

2. Pour batter on a greased pan.

3. Choose the air fry function.

4. Set temperature to 320°F.

5. Air fry for 12 minutes or until the toothpick comes out clean when the center is poked.

Serving suggestion

Let the cake cool for a few minutes then spread the chocolate frosting.

Tip

Garnish with cherries.

Air Fryer Strawberry Shortcake

Preparation time
20 MINUTES

Cooking time
20 MINUTES

Servings
6

Ratings

Ingredients

1 tablespoon vanilla extract

1 white cake mix

2 cups heavy cream

32 oz. fresh strawberries, diced

1/4 cup sugar

Nutritional Info

Calories: 230kcal

Carbs: 34g

Fat: 10g,

Protein: 3g.

Directions

1. Follow the instructions on the cake mix.
2. Pour batter into a greased pan.
3. Choose the bake function.
4. Bake for 20 minutes at 320°F.
5. In a mixing bowl, combine vanilla and heavy cream.
6. Add sugar and mix until frothy.
7. Cut the cake crosswise.
8. Put a layer of strawberries on top of the bottom half of the cake.
9. Then a layer of cream filling.
10. Place the other half of the cake on top of the filling.
11. Add another layer of filling.
12. Finally, decorate the top with strawberries.

Serving suggestion

Garnish with mint leaves on top.

Tip

Using non-stick cooking oil, grease your baking pan.

Upside Down Pineapple Cake

Preparation time
15 MINUTES

Cooking time
25 MINUTES

Servings
6

Ratings

Ingredients

1/4 cup brown sugar

1 package yellow cake mix

2 tablespoons melted butter

2-3 maraschino cherries

20 oz. can pineapple slices

Ingredients needed to make cake mix

Nutritional Info

Calories: 390kcal

Carbs: 56g

Fat: 17.2g,

Protein: 3.7g.

Directions

1. Spray the bottom of the baking pan with non-stick spray.
2. Melt butter in the microwave and pour it on the baking pan bottom.
3. Next, sprinkle brown sugar on top of melted butter.
4. Put the pineapples on top of the sugar.
5. Add cherries in the pineapple holes.
6. Follow the instructions on the cake mix box to make the batter.
7. On top of pineapples, pour batter in the pan.
8. Choose the bake function.
9. Bake for 25 minutes at 320°F.

Serving suggestion

Let the cake cool down before flipping the pan.

Tip

Check the middle with a toothpick to see if the cake is done cooking. The ingredients will vary depending on the cake mix package you will use.

Easiest Air Fryer Brownies

Preparation time
5 MINUTES

Cooking time
15 MINUTES

Servings
4

Ratings

Ingredients

2 large eggs

1/4 teaspoon baking powder

1/2 cup all-purpose flour

1/4 cup unsalted butter, melted

6 tablespoons unsweetened cocoa powder

1/2 teaspoon vanilla extract

3/4 cup sugar

1 tablespoon vegetable oil

1/4 teaspoon salt

Nutritional Info

Calories: 335kcal

Carbs: 39g

Fat: 23g,

Protein: 8.2g.

Directions

1. Grease a 7-inch baking pan. Set aside.

2. Preheat air fryer to 330°F.

3. In a big mixing bowl, incorporate all of the ingredients and stir well.

4. Gently pour into pan.

5. Choose the bake function.

6. Bake for 15 minutes in the air fryer.

Serving suggestion

Let the brownie cool down before slicing and serving.

Tip

Garnish with powdered sugar.

Beef Dishes

Rib Eye Steak

 Preparation time
10 MINUTES

 Cooking time
10 MINUTES

 Servings
2

 Ratings

Ingredients

2 rib eye steaks

2 tablespoons butter, melted

Salt and pepper to taste

Directions

1. Brush steaks with melted butter.

2. Season with salt and pepper.

3. Preheat your air fryer oven to 400 degrees F.

4. Add the steaks to the air fryer oven.

5. Set it to air fry.

6. Cook at 5 minutes per side.

Serving suggestion

Let steak rest for 10 minutes before serving.

Tip

Let steaks sit at room temperature for 30 minutes before seasoning.

Beef Kebab

Preparation time
2 HOURS 15 MINUTES

Cooking time
5 MINUTES

Servings
8

Ratings

Ingredients

2 cups teriyaki sauce, divided

1-1/2 lb. sirloin steak, sliced into cubes

1 onion, diced

1 green bell pepper, sliced

Directions

1. Pour a portion of the teriyaki sauce into a plastic bag that can be sealed.
2. Add steak cubes to the bag.
3. Turn to coat evenly.
4. Refrigerate for 2 hours.
5. Thread steak cubes and vegetables onto skewers.
6. Brush with the remaining sauce.
7. Place in the air fryer oven.
8. Choose grill or roast option.
9. For 5 minutes cook at 400 degrees F per side.

Serving suggestion

Serve with remaining teriyaki sauce.

Tip

You can also use rib eye steak sliced into cubes.

Bourbon Steaks

 **Preparation time**
1 HOUR 10 MINUTES

 Cooking time
10 MINUTES

 Servings
4

Ratings

Ingredients

1 lb. steak, sliced into cubes

Marinade

1/2 cup vegetable oil
1/2 cup bourbon
1/2 cup Worcestershire sauce
1/2 cup mustard
1/2 cup brown sugar

Directions

1. Mix the marinade ingredients in a bowl.
2. Add the steak cubes to the marinade.
3. Refrigerate for 1 hour after covering to marinate.
4. Transfer steak cubes to the air fryer tray.
5. Select grill setting.
6. Set it to 400 degrees F.
7. Cook for 5 minutes.
8. Turn and cook for another 5 minutes.

Serving suggestion

Serve with vegetable side dish.

Tip

Honey can also be substituted for brown sugar.

Steak with Pastrami Butter

Preparation time
4 MINUTES

Cooking time
12 MINUTES

Servings
2

Ratings

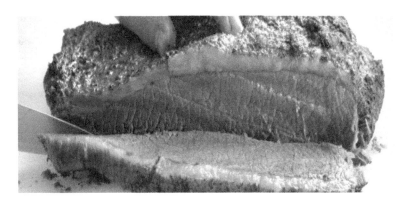

Ingredients

2 sirloin steaks
2 tablespoons butter
Salt and pepper to taste
1/4 cup butter
2 teaspoons pastrami spice blend

Directions

1. Preheat your air fryer oven to 400 degrees F for 5 minutes.

2. Spread 2 tablespoons butter on both sides of steaks.

3. Sprinkle with salt and pepper.

4. Place the steaks inside the air fryer oven.

5. Turn to air fry setting.

6. Cook steaks for 6 minutes per side.

7. Mix the butter and pastrami spice blend.

8. Serve on top of the steaks.

Serving suggestion

Serve with green leafy salad.

Tip

Let steak rest for 10 minutes at room temperature before seasoning.

Baked Meatballs

 Preparation time
10 MINUTES

 Cooking time
15 MINUTES

 Servings
4

Ratings

Ingredients

16 oz. frozen meatballs
14 oz. marinara sauce
1/2 cup mozzarella cheese

Directions

1. Spread marinara sauce on top of a baking pan.
2. Add meatballs on top.
3. Place the pan inside the air fryer oven.
4. Choose bake function.
5. Set it to 340 degrees F.
6. Cook for 10 minutes.
7. Sprinkle mozzarella cheese over the meatballs.
8. Cook for another 5 minutes.

Serving suggestion

Garnish with fresh basil leaves.

Tip

Use low-sodium marinara sauce.

Garlic Parmesan Strip Steak

Preparation time
20 MINUTES

Cooking time
10 MINUTES

Servings
2

Ratings

Ingredients

Steaks
2 strip steaks
1 teaspoon olive oil
Salt and pepper to taste
Garlic Parmesan butter
2 teaspoons garlic, minced
1/2 cup butter
1/4 cup Parmesan cheese, grated

Directions

1. With a brush add olive oil on both sides of the steaks.

2. Place inside the air fryer oven.

3. Select air fry option.

4. Air fry for 5 minutes per side.

5. Mix garlic, butter and cheese in a bowl.

6. Form butter mixture into a round shape.

7. Refrigerate until firm.

8. Top steaks with the butter.

Serving suggestion

Let rest for 5 minutes before serving.

Tip

Use New York strip steaks.

Parmesan Crusted Steak

Preparation time
3 MINUTES

Cooking time
12 MINUTES

Servings
4

Ratings

Ingredients

4 flank steaks

2 tablespoons olive oil

3 tablespoons Parmesan cheese, grated

Salt and pepper to taste

Directions

1. Rub steaks with olive oil.

2. Sprinkle both sides with Parmesan cheese, salt and pepper.

3. Add steaks to the air crisper tray.

4. Set your air fryer oven to air fry.

5. Cook for 6 minutes per side.

Serving suggestion

Garnish with parsley.

Tip

Dried herbs may also be added to the Parmesan mixture.

Seared Sirloin Steak

Preparation time
3 MINUTES

Cooking time
12 MINUTES

Servings
2

Ratings

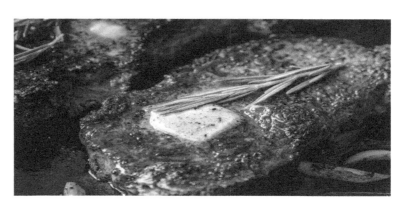

Ingredients

2 sirloin steaks
2 tablespoons olive oil
Salt and pepper to taste

Directions

1. Preheat your air fryer oven to 400 degrees F for 5 minutes.

2. Select air fry setting.

3. Coat steaks with olive oil.

4. Sprinkle with salt and pepper.

5. Place steaks in the air crisper tray.

6. Cook for 6 minutes per side.

Serving suggestion

Serve with roasted baby potatoes.

Tip

You can also season with dried rosemary.

Cranberry Meatballs

Preparation time
10 MINUTES

Cooking time
10 MINUTES

Servings
6

Ratings

Ingredients

28 oz. frozen meatballs
12 oz. chili sauce
14 oz. cranberry sauce

Directions

1. Select air fry setting in your air fryer oven.

2. Cook meatballs at 350 degrees F for 5 minutes, turning once.

3. In a bowl, mix chili sauce and cranberry sauce.

4. Pour sauce into a pan over medium heat.

5. Heat for 10 minutes.

6. Toss meatballs in sauce and serve.

Serving suggestion

Garnish with chopped scallions.

Tip

Insert toothpicks if serving as appetizer.

Pepper and Thyme Steak

 Preparation time
10 MINUTES

 Cooking time
20 MINUTES

 Servings
4

Ratings

Ingredients

2 tablespoons olive oil
1 teaspoon thyme, chopped
1 tablespoon lemon zest
4 tablespoons soy sauce
Salt and pepper to taste
1 lb. flank steak

Directions

1. Combine all the ingredients except flank steak in a bowl.

2. Brush both sides of steaks with this mixture.

3. Place steaks inside the air fryer oven.

4. Select roast function.

5. Cook at 400 degrees F for 7 to 10 minutes per side.

Serving suggestion

Serve with salad.

Tip

Add 2 more minutes cooking time for well done.

Greek Burger

Preparation time
10 MINUTES

Cooking time
10 MINUTES

Servings
4

Ratings

Ingredients

1-1/2 lb. ground beef

1 clove garlic, minced

1 tablespoon fresh oregano, chopped

1/2 cup feta cheese

1 tablespoon lemon juice

Directions

1. Combine all ingredients in a bowl.

2. Form patties from the mixture.

3. Add these to the air fryer oven.

4. Choose air fry setting.

5. For 5 minutes per side cook at 380 degrees F.

Serving suggestion

Serve in burger buns with lettuce and tomatoes.

Tip

You can swap garlic with garlic powder.

Bacon Wrapped Beef Tenderloin

 Preparation time
5 MINUTES

 Cooking time
12 MINUTES

 Servings
2

Ratings

Ingredients

2 beef tenderloin fillets

Salt and pepper to taste

2 slices bacon

Directions

1. Season beef with salt and pepper.

2. Wrap bacon around the beef.

3. Set your air fryer oven to air fry.

4. For 6 minutes per side cook at 400 degrees F.

Serving suggestion

Drizzle with steak sauce before serving.

Tip

Use a toothpick to secure the bacon.

Blue Cheese Burger

 Preparation time
5 MINUTES

 Cooking time
15 MINUTES

 Servings
15

Ratings

Ingredients

3 lb. lean ground beef

1/8 cup chives, minced

4 oz. blue cheese

1 teaspoon Worcestershire sauce

1/4 teaspoon hot pepper sauce

Salt and pepper to taste

Directions

1. Combine all the ingredients in a bowl.

2. Form patties from the mixture.

3. Add patties to the air fryer oven.

4. Cook the patties at 360 degrees F for 6 minutes.

5. Flip and cook for another 5 to 7 minutes.

Serving suggestion

Serve in burger buns with lettuce and tomatoes.

Tip

Make sure burger patty is fully cooked. Extend cooking time if necessary.

Hoisin Meatballs

Preparation time
5 MINUTES

Cooking time
12 MINUTES

Servings
6

Ratings

Ingredients

1 lb. lean ground beef
2 tablespoons scallions, chopped
2 tablespoons ginger, minced
1 teaspoon sugar
2 teaspoons garlic powder
1 egg, beaten
1/2 cup breadcrumbs
1/2 cup hoisin sauce
Cooking spray

Directions

1. Mix all the ingredients except hoisin sauce in a bowl.

2. Form meatballs from the mixture.

3. Spray with oil.

4. Transfer to the air fryer oven.

5. Select roast setting.

6. Cook at 350 degrees F for 6 minutes per side.

7. Toss in hoisin sauce and serve.

Serving suggestion

Garnish with toasted sesame seeds.

Tip

Use lean ground beef.

Fried Steak

Preparation time
20 MINUTES

Cooking time
10 MINUTES

Servings
4

Ratings

Ingredients

4 steaks
Salt and pepper to taste
1 cup flour
1 egg, beaten
1/4 cup milk
1 cup breadcrumbs
Cooking spray

Directions

1. Season steaks with salt and pepper.

2. Cover with flour.

3. Dip in egg mixed with milk.

4. Dredge with breadcrumbs.

5. Spray with oil.

6. Place steaks in the air fryer tray.

7. Choose air fry setting.

8. For 5 minutes per side cook at 400 degrees F.

Serving suggestion

Serve with mashed potatoes and gravy.

Tip

Use prime rib or rib eye steaks.

Steak Cubes with Barbecue Sauce

 Preparation time
5 MINUTES

 Cooking time
10 MINUTES

 Servings
4

Ratings

Ingredients

1 lb. steak, sliced into cubes

1 cup barbecue sauce

Directions

1. Toss the steak cubes in the sauce.

2. Spread in the air fryer tray.

3. Choose air fry setting.

4. For 5 minutes per side cook at 400 degrees F.

5. Set oven to broil.

6. Increase temperature to 450 degrees F.

7. Cook for 2 minutes.

Serving suggestion

Season with pepper before serving.

Tip

Spread steak cubes in a single layer.

Beef and Spinach Rolls

Preparation time
5 MINUTES

Cooking time
12 MINUTES

Servings
2

Ratings

Ingredients

2 beef tenderloin fillets

Salt and pepper to taste

1 cup spinach, sliced

1/2 cup garlic herb cream cheese

Directions

1. Season beef with salt and pepper.

2. In a bowl, mix spinach and garlic herb cream cheese.

3. Spread mixture on top of the beef.

4. Roll up the beef.

5. Place in the air fryer tray.

6. Choose air fry setting.

7. Set it to 400 degrees F.

8. Cook for 6 minutes per side.

Serving suggestion

Serve with green salad.

Tip

Flatten beef with meat mallet.

Bread Bagel
and Pizza

Cheddar Jalapeno Cornbread

Preparation time
10 MINUTES

Cooking time
30 MINUTES

Servings
6

Ratings

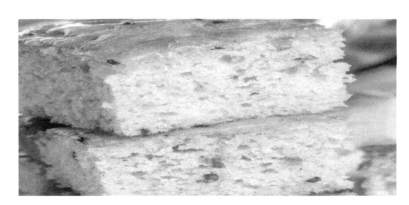

Ingredients

1-1/2 cup all-purpose flour
1-1/2 cup yellow cornmeal
1-1/5 tbsp. baking powder
1-1/2 tbsp. salt
1-1/2 cup whole milk
1/4 tbsp. cayenne pepper, ground
3 eggs
1/2 cup sharp cheddar
1-1/2 tbsp. green jalapeno, minced
1-1/2 tbsp. red jalapeno, minced
1/3 cup vegetable oil plus 1 tbsp. vegetable oil
1-1/2 tbsp. honey
1/2 tbsp. butter

Nutritional Info

Calories: 201kcal
Carbs: 27g
Fat: 8.2g,
Protein: 6g

Directions

1. In a mixing bowl, mix flour, cornmeal, baking powder, salt, and pepper until well combined.

2. In another bowl, mix milk, eggs, cheese, jalapenos, and 1/3 cup vegetable oil.

3. Incorporate the dry and wet ingredients in a mixing bowl. Grease a baking pan with the remaining oil and pour the mixture.

4. Slide the pizza rack on shelf position 5 of the Emeril Lagasse Power Air Fryer 360 and place the baking pan on top.

5. Select the bake setting. Set the temperature knob to 325°F for 30 minutes. Press start.

6. Cook until the toothpick comes out clean when inserted in the bread.

7. Brush the bread with honey and butter, then let rest to cool before serving.

Family Banana Nut Bread

Preparation time
10 MINUTES

Cooking time
1 HOUR 15 MINUTES

Servings
10

Ratings

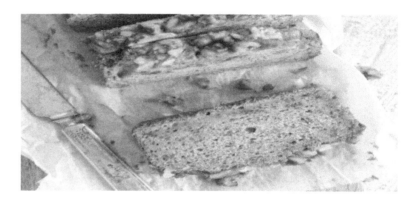

Ingredients

8 oz. cream cheese, softened

1 cup white sugar

1/2 cup butter

2 eggs, beaten

2 ripe bananas, mashed

2-1/4 cups all-purpose flour

1/2 tbsp. baking soda

1-1/2 tbsp. baking powder

1 cup walnuts, chopped

Nutritional Info

Calories: 449kcal

Carbs: 49.3g

Fat: 26g,

Protein: 8g

Directions

1. Beat cream cheese, sugar, butter, eggs, and mashed banana in a mixing bowl until well mixed and smooth.

2. Stir with flour, baking soda, baking powder, and walnuts until well combined. Pour the batter on a greased loaf pan.

3. Slide the pizza rack on shelf position 5 and place the loaf pan on top.

4. Select the bake setting on the Emeril Lagasse Power Air Fryer 360 and set the temperature knob at 350°F for 75 minutes. Press start

5. Allow 10 minutes for the bread to cool before serving.

Basic Fruit Bread

Preparation time
15 MINUTES

Cooking time
35 MINUTES

Servings
6

Ratings

Ingredients

3 cups all-purpose flour

2 tbsp. baking powder

1 tbsp. baking soda

1/2 tbsp. salt

1 cup white sugar

1/2 cup vegetable oil

2 eggs

1 cup apple, shredded

3/4 cup walnuts, chopped

1/2 tbsp. vanilla extract

Nutritional Info

Calories: 391kcal

Carbs: 52g

Fat: 18g,

Protein: 7g

Directions

1. In a mixing pan, mix flour, baking powder, baking soda, salt, white sugar, vegetable oil, eggs, apple, walnuts, and vanilla extract until moistened

2. Grease the loaf pan and pour the mixture on it.

3. Slide the pizza rack on shelf position 5 of the Emeril Lagasse Power Air Fryer 360 and place the loaf pan on top.

4. Select the bake setting. Set the temperature knob at 350°F for 35 minutes. Press start.

5. Let the bread cool before serving.

Mini Pizza with Italian Sausage

Preparation time
20 MINUTES

Cooking time
30 MINUTES

Servings
4

Ratings

★ ★ ★

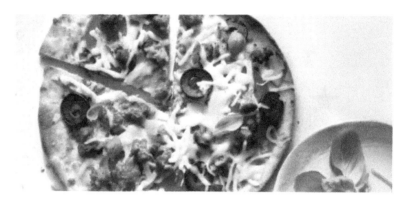

Ingredients

1 lb. pizza dough

1-1/2 lb. Hot Italian Sausage

3-1/2 tomato sauce

8 oz. mozzarella cheese

2 tbsp. thyme leaves, freshly chopped

1/2 tbsp. red pepper, crushed

1/4 cup Parmigiano-Reggiano, finely grated

Extra virgin oil

Nutritional Info

Calories: 130kcal

Carbs: 13g

Fat: 5g,

Protein: 6g

Directions

1. On a work surface that is floured, cut the dough into four equal parts. Roll each dough on the work surface into an 8 inches round.

2. Place the sausage on the crisper tray and slide the tray on position 2 of the Emeril Lagasse Power Air Fryer 360.

3. Select the air fry setting and set the temperature knob at 400°F for 15 minutes. Press start.

4. Transfer the dough to the crisper tray and spoon the tomato sauce on each dough surface. Sprinkle cheese, top with the sausage, and garnish with thyme, pepper, and Parmigiano-Reggiano.

5. Slide the crisper tray on shelf position 2. Select the pizza setting. Set the temperature knob at 425°F for 20 minutes. Press start.

6. Repeat the cycle with the remaining 3 pizzas. Serve the pizza drizzled with olive oil.

Roasted Garlic Pizza with Garlic Sauce

 Preparation time
30 MINUTES

 Cooking time
20 MINUTES

 Servings
8

Ratings

Ingredients

2 tbsp. butter, unsalted
2 tbsp. all-purpose flour
1 cup whole milk
1/4 tbsp. cayenne pepper, ground
3 heads garlic
1/4 tbsp. salt
1 cup of warm water
1 tbsp. honey
2 tbsp. olive oil
1-1/4 oz. active dry yeast
2-1/2 cup all-purpose flour
8 oz. mozzarella cheese
4 oz. fontina cheese, grated
1/2 cup Parmigiano- Reggiano
cheese, finely grated
30 pieces tomatoes, sun-dried
2 tbsp. basil leaves, freshly
chopped

Nutritional Info

Calories: 280kcal
Carbs: 34g
Fat: 11g,
Protein: 12g

Directions

1. In a saucepan, melt the butter and cook the all-purpose flour for 3 minutes.

2. Whisk in milk until thickened. Add pepper, garlic, and salt then simmer for 15 minutes on low heat to make the bechamel.

3. In a mixing bowl, mix warm water honey, and oil. Mix in the yeast, flour, and salt to the bowl. Knead until smooth. Let rest for 20 minutes.

4. Divide the pizza dough into half and roll it to make it fit the pizza rack.

5. Top with cheeses and tomatoes. Slide the pizza rack on position 5 and select the pizza setting on the Emeril Lagasse Power Air Fryer 360.

6. Set the temperature knob at 425°F for 20 minutes. Press start.

7. Repeat with the second pizza. Top the pizza with parsley, basil, and red pepper.

Four Cheese Margherita Pizza

Preparation time
25 MINUTES

Cooking time
15 MINUTES

Servings
8

Ratings

Ingredients

1/4 cup olive oil

1 tbsp. garlic, raw

1/2 tbsp. salt

8 Roma tomatoes

2 pizza crust

8 oz. mozzarella cheese

4 oz. fontina cheese

10 fresh basil

1/2 cup parmesan cheese, grated

1/2 cup feta cheese

Nutritional Info

Calories: 551kcal

Carbs: 54g

Fat: 18g,

Protein: 29g

Directions

1. Mix the oil, garlic, and salt in a mixing bowl. Add in the tomatoes and set aside for 15 minutes.

2. Place the crust on the crisper tray and brush it with tomato marinade, then sprinkle mozzarella and fontina cheese.

3. Arrange the tomatoes on top then sprinkle basil, parmesan cheese, and feta cheese.

4. Slide the crisper tray on shelf position 2 of the Emeril Lagasse Power Air Fryer 360 and select the pizza setting. Set the temperature knob at 400°F for 15 minutes. Press start.

5. Cook the cheese for about 5 mins or until it is golden brown and bubbly. Repeat the cycle with the remaining pizza.

6. Serve the pizza and enjoy it.

Satay Chicken Pizza

Preparation time
15 MINUTES

Cooking time
12 MINUTES

Servings
4

Ingredients

1 tbsp. vegetable corn oil

2 chicken breasts

4 small pita bread

1 cup peanut sauce

1 bunch spring onions

4 slices provolone cheese

Nutritional Info

Calories: 391kcal

Carbs: 52g

Fat: 18g,

Protein: 7g

Directions

1. Heat oil in a nonstick skillet and sauté the chicken for 7 minutes.

2. Spoon peanut sauce on each pita bread the sprinkle the cooked chicken. Add scallions and a slice of cheese.

3. Place the pizza on a crisper tray lined with a cookie sheet.

4. Slide the crisper tray on shelf position 2 of the Emeril Lagasse Power Air Fryer 360.Select the pizza setting. Set the temperature knob at 400°F for 12 minutes. Press start.

5. Let the pizza cool for 2 minutes before cutting and serving.

Black and White Pizza

 Preparation time
15 MINUTES

 Cooking time
15 MINUTES

 Servings
4

Ratings

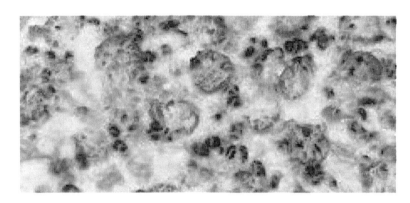

Ingredients

1 tbsp. olive oil

1/2 garlic clove, raw

6 oz. chicken

2 prepared pizza crust

1 cup Di Giorno Alfredo sauce

6 0z packed mozzarella cheese

1/2 cup beans

4 oz. jalapeno peppers

1 tbsp. dried parsley

Nutritional Info

Calories: 731kcal

Carbs: 61g

Fat: 38g,

Protein: 41g

Directions

1. Heat oil in a nonstick skillet over medium heat. Cook garlic until fragrant then add chicken and cook until heated through.

2. Spread Alfredo sauce on the pizza crust, then sprinkle some cheese.

3. Arrange chicken strips over the cheese then add black beans. Place peppers on top.

4. Add the remaining cheese then garnish with parsley. Place the pizza on a crisper tray of the Emeril Lagasse Power Air Fryer 360.

5. Slide the crisper tray on shelf position 2. Select the pizza setting. Set the temperature knob at 450°F for 15 minutes. Press start.

6. Cook until the crust is crispy and the cheese has melted.

Bread Machine Bagels

Preparation time
25 MINUTES

Cooking time
25 MINUTES

Servings
6

Ratings

Ingredients

1 cup of water
1-1/2 tbsp. salt
2 tbsp. sugar
3 cups wheat flour
2-1/4 tbsp. yeast
3 quarts water
3 tbsp. granulated sugar
1 tbsp. cornmeal
1 egg
3 tbsp. poppy seeds

Nutritional Info

Calories: 50kcal
Carbs: 9g
Fat: 1.3g,
Protein: 1.4g

Directions

1. Place water, sugar, salt, flour, and yeast in a bread machine. Select dough setting.

2. On a surface that is floured, Put the dough to rest for a few minutes.

3. Meanwhile, bring water to boil then stir with sugar. Cut dough into nine pieces and roll each into a ball.

4. Flatten and poke a hole on the ball using your hands. Cover the bagels and let rest for 10 minutes.

5. Sprinkle cornmeal on a baking sheet then transfer the bagels to boiling water. Let boil for 1 minute then drain them on a clean paper towel.

6. Arrange the bagels on a baking sheet then glaze them with egg and sprinkle poppy seeds.

7. Place the baking sheet on the pizza rack of the Emeril Lagasse Power Air Fryer 360 and Select the bake setting. Set the temperature knob at 375°F for 25 minutes. Press start.

8. The bagels should be well browned and cooked.

Bagel and Cheese Bake

 Preparation time
30 MINUTES

 Cooking time
30 MINUTES

 Servings
12

Ratings

Ingredients

1/2 lb. pork
1/2 cup onions, raw
3 bagels
1 cup cheddar cheese
12 eggs
2 cups of milk, reduced fat
2 tbsp. parsley
1/4 tbsp. black pepper
1/2 cup parmesan cheese, grated

Nutritional Info

Calories: 249kcal
Carbs: 15g
Fat: 13.5g,
Protein: 17g

Directions

1. Cook bacon and onion in a nonstick skillet and cook over medium heat until well browned. Drain and set aside.

2. Slice the bagel into 6 slices then arrange them on a greased baking dish. Cover the bagels with bacon and onion mixture then top with cheese.

3. In a mixing bowl, whisk together eggs, milk, parsley, and pepper. Pour the egg mixture on the bagels and refrigerate overnight while covered.

4. Place the baking sheet on the pizza rack of the Emeril Lagasse Power Air Fryer 360 and select the bake setting. Set the temperature knob at 400°F for 30 minutes. Press start.

5. Sprinkle parmesan cheese and serve when warm. Enjoy.

Pork Dishes

Breaded Pork Chops

Preparation time
10 MINUTES

Cooking time
10 MINUTES

Servings
4

Ratings

Ingredients

4 pork chops
Salt and pepper to taste
1 egg, beaten
1/2 cup cornflake crumbs
1 cup breadcrumbs
1 teaspoon chili powder
2 teaspoons sweet paprika
1 teaspoon onion powder
1 teaspoon garlic powder

Directions

1. Season pork chops with salt and pepper.

2. Dip in egg.

3. In a bowl, mi the remaining ingredients.

4. Dredge pork chops with breadcrumb mixture.

5. For 10 minutes Air fry at 400°F.

Serving suggestion

Serve with garlic mustard dip.

Tip

Use boneless pork chops.

Crispy Pork Belly

 Preparation time
10 MINUTES

 Cooking time
30 MINUTES

 Servings
4

Ratings

Ingredients

1 lb. pork belly, sliced into 3
2 tablespoons olive oil
Salt to taste

Directions

1. Coat pork belly with oil.

2. Season with salt.

3. Place in the air fryer tray.

4. For 20 minutes cook at 350°F.

5. Increase temperature to 400°F.

6. Cook for 10 minutes.

Serving suggestion

Garnish with basil leaves.

Tip

The Pork belly may also be cut into smaller pieces.

Chili Cheese Dog

Preparation time
20 MINUTES

Cooking time
10 MINUTES

Servings
4

Ratings

Ingredients

4 hotdogs

4 hotdog rolls

1 cup chili

1/2 cup cheddar cheese, shredded

Directions

1. Air fry the hot dogs at 370°F for 5 minutes.

2. Place the hot dogs in the buns.

3. Pour chili on top of the hot dogs.

4. Sprinkle cheese on top.

5. Air fry at 300°F for 5 minutes or until cheese has melted.

Serving suggestion

Sprinkle with pepper before serving.

Tip

You can also use cheese dogs.

Sausage and Cheese Egg Scramble

 Preparation time
2 MINUTES

 Cooking time
13 MINUTES

 Servings
4

Ratings

Ingredients

6 eggs

3/4 cup milk

6 sausages, cooked and crumbled

1 cup cheddar cheese, shredded

Cooking spray

Directions

1. Whisk the eggs in a bowl and stir in the milk, sausages and cheese.

2. Spray your air fryer tray with oil.

3. Pour the mixture into the ramekins.

4. Add ramekins to the air fryer tray.

5. For 8 minutes cook at 320°F.

6. Check if the eggs are done.

7. Cook for another 5 minutes.

Serving suggestion

Sprinkle chopped scallions on top.

Tip

Herbs may be added to the mixture as well.

Thyme Pork Chops

 Preparation time
3 MINUTES

 Cooking time
12 MINUTES

 Servings
4

Ratings

Ingredients

4 pork chops
4 teaspoons dried thyme
Salt and pepper to taste
2 eggs, beaten
1 cup cornstarch
Cooking spray

Directions

1. Season pork chops with thyme, salt and pepper.
2. Dip pork chops in eggs.
3. Cover with cornstarch.
4. Spray with oil.
5. Add to the air fryer tray.
6. Cook at 360°F for 6 minutes per side.

Serving suggestion

Serve with salad made of shredded purple cabbage.

Tip

You can also use other herbs to season the pork chops.

Honey Garlic Pork Chops

Preparation time
5 MINUTES

Cooking time
14 MINUTES

Servings
4

Ratings

Ingredients

4 pork chops

Salt and pepper to taste

4 tablespoons olive oil

4 cloves garlic, minced

1/2 cup honey

2 tablespoons sweet chili sauce

4 tablespoons lemon juice

Directions

1. Season pork chops with salt and pepper.

2. Add to the air fryer tray.

3. Cook at 400°F for 7 minutes per side.

4. Pour olive oil into a pan over medium heat.

5. Cook garlic for 1 minute, stirring often.

6. Stir in the remaining ingredients.

7. Simmer for 10 minutes.

8. Pour sauce over the pork chops and serve.

Serving suggestion

Sprinkle with pepper.

Tip

Use bone-in pork chops.

Ham with Apricot Sauce

 Preparation time
5 MINUTES

 Cooking time
10 MINUTES

Servings
2

Ratings

Ingredients

1/4 cup apricot jam
1 teaspoon mustard
1 teaspoon lemon juice
1/2 teaspoon ground cinnamon
2 ham steaks

Directions

1. Combine apricot jam, mustard, lemon juice and cinnamon in a bowl.

2. Brush sauce on both sides of ham.

3. Place the ham on the air fryer tray.

4. Cook at 350°F for 5 minutes.

5. Flip and brush with the remaining sauce.

6. Cook for another 5 minutes.

Serving suggestion

Garnish with lemon wedges.

Tip

Use Dijon mustard.

Baby Back Ribs

 Preparation time
5 MINUTES

 Cooking time
30 MINUTES

 Servings
4

Ratings

★ ★ ★

Ingredients

1 rack baby back ribs

Dry rub

2 tablespoons olive oil
1/2 teaspoon ground paprika
1 tablespoon brown sugar
1 tablespoon ground cumin
1 teaspoon chili powder
1/2 teaspoon garlic powder
2 teaspoons liquid smoke
Salt and pepper to taste

Directions

1. Mix the dry rub ingredients.

2. Rub it on all sides of ribs.

3. Add the ribs to the air fryer.

4. Cook at 400°F for 20 minutes.

5. Flip and cook for another 10 minutes.

Serving suggestion

Serve with ketchup and mustard.

Tip

Extend cooking time if not fully done after 30 minutes.

Sausages Onions and Peppers

Preparation time
5 MINUTES

Cooking time
8 MINUTES

Servings
4

Ratings

Ingredients

1 onion, sliced

2 red bell peppers, sliced

2 tablespoons olive oil

1 tablespoon Italian seasoning

1 lb. Italian sausages

Directions

1. Combine all the ingredients except sausages in a bowl.

2. Add mixture to the air fryer tray.

3. Add sausages on top of the vegetables.

4. Cook at 400°F for 5 minutes.

5. Turn sausages and cook for another 3 minutes.

Serving suggestion

Serve with mustard.

Tip

You can also add green bell pepper and yellow bell pepper.

Pork Cabbage and Mushrooms

 Preparation time
5 MINUTES

 Cooking time
10 MINUTES

 Servings
4

Ratings

Ingredients

1 lb. pork tenderloin

1 tablespoon Cajun seasoning

Salt and pepper to taste

1/2 cup onion, chopped

10 oz. Cremini mushrooms, diced

2 red bell peppers, diced

1 lb. cabbage, shredded

2 tablespoons olive oil

Directions

1. Season pork with Cajun seasoning, salt and pepper.

2. Add to the air fryer tray.

3. Cook at 350°F for 5 minutes per side.

4. Toss veggies in oil.

5. Add to the air fryer tray along with the pork.

6. Cook for another 5 minutes.

Serving suggestion

Drizzle with cooking liquid.

Tip

You can also add garlic powder to the seasoning mixture.

Paprika Pork Chops

Preparation time
5 MINUTES

Cooking time
14 MINUTES

Servings
4

Ratings

Ingredients

4 pork chops
2 tablespoons olive oil
2 tablespoon garlic salt
1 teaspoon smoked paprika
Salt and pepper to taste

Directions

1. Brush pork chops with oil.

2. Sprinkle with garlic salt, paprika, salt and pepper.

3. Air fry the pork at 380°F for 7 minutes.

4. Turn and cook for another 7 minutes.

Serving suggestion

Serve with herbed boiled potatoes.

Tip

Internal temperature should be 145°F.

Pepper Pork Chops

Preparation time
5 MINUTES

Cooking time
5 MINUTES

Servings
4

Ratings

Ingredients

4 pork chops
2 to 3 teaspoons black pepper
Cooking spray

Directions

1. Start by flattening your pork on a cutting board.

2. Season with salt and pepper.

3. Cook at 320°F for 5 minutes per side.

Serving suggestion

Garnish with fresh herbs.

Tip

Flatten pork chops with meat mallet before seasoning.

Crispy Pork Strips

Preparation time
10 MINUTES

Cooking time
10 MINUTES

Servings
3

Ratings

Ingredients

3 pork fillets, sliced into strips

2 teaspoons olive oil

1 teaspoon garlic powder

1 teaspoon paprika

Salt and pepper to taste

1 egg

1 cup breadcrumbs

Directions

1. Coat pork strips with oil.

2. Season with garlic powder, paprika, salt and pepper.

3. Dip in eggs.

4. Cover with breadcrumbs.

5. Cook at 350°F for 5 minutes per side.

Serving suggestion

Serve with dip of choice.

Tip

Cook in batches so as not to overcrowd the air fryer.

Pork and Green Beans

 Preparation time
15 MINUTES

 Cooking time
15 MINUTES

 Servings
4

Ratings

Ingredients

1/4 cup almond flour

1 teaspoon Creole seasoning

1/4 cup Parmesan cheese, grated

1 teaspoon paprika

1 teaspoon garlic powder

4 pork chops

4 cups green beans, trimmed and steamed

Cooking spray

Directions

1. Preheat your air fryer to 375°F.

2. Spray your air fryer tray with oil.

3. In a bowl, introduce all the ingredients except pork chops and green beans.

4. Spray pork chops with oil.

5. Coat with spice mixture.

6. Air fry for 15 minutes, turning once.

Serving suggestion

Serve with ketchup and hot sauce.

Tip

You can also sprinkle green beans with Parmesan cheese before serving.

Pork and Potatoes

 Preparation time
5 MINUTES

 Cooking time
12 MINUTES

 Servings
2

Ratings

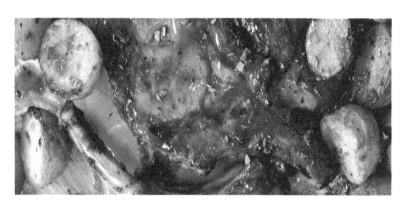

Ingredients

2 pork chops
1 tablespoons oil
1 tablespoons steak seasoning
1 teaspoon paprika
2 cups French fries, cooked

Directions

1. For 5 minutes Preheat your air fryer to 400°F.

2. Brush pork chops with oil.

3. Season with steak seasoning and paprika.

4. Air fry for 6 to 8 minutes per side.

5. Serve with French fries.

Serving suggestion

Garnish with lemon wedges and chopped scallions.

Tip

Use pork chops that are at least 1 ½ inch thick.

Pork and Mushroom Bites

 Preparation time
10 MINUTES

 Cooking time
20 MINUTES

 Servings
4

Ratings

Ingredients

1 lb. pork fillet, sliced into cubes

8 oz. mushrooms

1 teaspoon Worcestershire sauce

2 tablespoons butter, melted

1/2 teaspoon garlic powder

Salt and pepper to taste

Directions

1. For 5 minutes Preheat your air fryer to 400°F.

2. Toss all the ingredients in a bowl.

3. Transfer to the air fryer tray.

4. Cook at 400°F for 20 minutes, turning twice.

Serving suggestion

Serve with dip of choice.

Tip

Extend cooking time if you want your pork more well done.

Pork and Brussels Sprouts

 Preparation time
15 MINUTES

 Cooking time
15 MINUTES

 Servings
4

Ratings

Ingredients

8 pork chops
Cooking spray
Salt and pepper to taste
1 teaspoon olive oil
1 teaspoon mustard
1 teaspoon maple syrup
6 oz. Brussels sprouts, sliced

Directions

1. Spray your pork chops with oil.
2. Season with salt and pepper.
3. In a bowl, mix the remaining ingredients.
4. Add pork chops to the air fryer.
5. Cook for 5 minutes per side.
6. Transfer to a plate.
7. Add Brussels sprouts to the air fryer.
8. Cook for 3 minutes.

Serving suggestion

Season with pepper before serving.

Tip

Use Dijon style mustard.

Fish and
Seafood Dishes

Broiled Scallops and Shrimp

Preparation time
MINUTES

Cooking time
MINUTES

Servings
6

Ratings

Ingredients

1/4 cup butter, melted

1 tablespoon lemon juice

1 tablespoon Worcestershire sauce

1/3 cup dry white wine

3 cloves garlic, crushed

Pinch red pepper flakes

Salt and pepper to taste

1 lb. shrimp, peeled and deveined

1 lb. scallops

1 cup cherry tomatoes, sliced in half

5 oz. baby spinach

Directions

1. Combine butter, lemon juice, Worcestershire sauce, wine, garlic, red pepper, salt and pepper in a bowl.

2. Toss shrimp and scallops in the bowl.

3. Transfer to the air fryer oven.

4. Choose broil setting.

5. Broil for 3 minutes.

6. Stir in tomatoes and spinach.

7. Broil for another 2 minutes.

Serving suggestion

Serve with slices of French bread.

Tip

You can also use other leafy greens in place of spinach.

Garlic Roasted Seafood

Preparation time
25 MINUTES

Cooking time
15 MINUTES

Servings
4

Ratings

Ingredients

1/2 cup butter

3 cloves garlic, crushed

1 tablespoon lemon juice

2 teaspoons lemon zest

1 teaspoon smoked paprika

1 cup shrimp, peeled and deveined

2 squids, cleaned

12 mussels

2 cups baby potatoes

2 cobs corn, sliced

Directions

1. Combine butter, garlic, lemon juice, lemon zest and paprika in a bowl.

2. Arrange the seafood in a baking pan.

3. Drizzle with the butter sauce.

4. Place inside the air fryer oven.

5. Select roast option.

6. For 15 minutes cook at 400 degrees F, stirring once or twice.

Serving suggestion

Sprinkle with chopped parsley.

Tip

Throw away mussels that did not open during cooking.

Grilled Tilapia

Preparation time
35 MINUTES

Cooking time
15 MINUTES

Servings
2

Ratings

Ingredients

1 tilapia

Marinade

2 tablespoons oil
5 cloves garlic
1 onion, sliced
1/2 teaspoon curry powder
2 seasoning cubes
2 sprigs fresh thyme
1 teaspoon nutmeg
Salt and pepper to taste

Directions

1. Add marinade ingredients to a blender.
2. Process until smooth.
3. Make several slits on both sides of fish.
4. Coat with the marinade.
5. Cover and refrigerate for 30 minutes.
6. Place the fish inside the air fryer oven.
7. Select grill setting.
8. Cook at 350 degrees F for 15 minutes per side.

Serving suggestion

Serve on top of leafy greens and sliced tomatoes.

Tip

You can also add chili powder to the marinade.

Bacon Wrapped Scallops

 Preparation time
15 MINUTES

 Cooking time
5 MINUTES

 Servings
4

Ratings

Ingredients

16 scallops
8 slices bacon, sliced into 2
1/4 teaspoon paprika
Pinch pepper

Directions

1. Wrap the scallops with bacon slices.
2. Secure with toothpicks.
3. Season with pepper and paprika.
4. Preheat your air fryer oven to 350 degrees F.
5. Choose air fry setting.
6. Cook for 3 minutes.
7. Flip and cook for another 3 minutes.

Serving suggestion

Serve immediately.

Tip

You can also pre-cook bacon by air frying at 400 degrees F for 3 minutes before wrapping it around the scallop.

Baked Lemon Butter Fish

Preparation time
5 MINUTES

Cooking time
12 MINUTES

Servings
4

Ratings

Ingredients

4 white fish fillets
1/4 cup butter, melted
3 cloves garlic, minced
2 tablespoons lemon juice
1 teaspoon lemon zest
Salt and pepper to taste
Lemon slices

Directions

1. Choose bake option in your air fryer oven.

2. Preheat it to 425 degrees F.

3. Arrange the fish fillets in a baking pan.

4. Combine the remaining ingredients except lemon slices in a bowl.

5. Pour the mixture over the fish.

6. Top with the lemon slices.

7. Bake in the air fryer oven for 6 minutes per side.

Serving suggestion

Garnish with chopped parsley.

Tip

You can also use garlic powder instead of minced garlic.

Baked Miso Tuna

 Preparation time
1 HOUR

 Cooking time
15 MINUTES

 Servings
4

Ratings

Ingredients

2 tuna steaks
1/2 tablespoon miso paste
2 tablespoons mirin
1 tablespoon garlic, minced
1 teaspoon rice wine
1/2 teaspoon vinegar

Directions

1. Add tuna steaks to a baking pan.
2. Combine remaining ingredients in a bowl.
3. Pour the marinade over the tuna.
4. Cover and refrigerate for 1 hour.
5. Transfer to the air fryer oven.
6. Choose bake setting.
7. Cook at 360 degrees F for 5 to 7 minutes per side.

Serving suggestion

Garnish with chopped green onion.

Tip

Tuna steaks should be at least ½ inch thick.

Tuna Casserole

Preparation time
5 MINUTES

Cooking time
10 MINUTES

Servings
2

Ratings

Ingredients

Casserole

10 oz. canned tuna flakes, drained

1/4 cup Mexican cheese blend, shredded

1/4 cup onion, chopped

1/4 teaspoon onion powder

1/4 cup celery, chopped

2 tablespoons mayonnaise

1/4 cup breadcrumbs

1 tablespoon Parmesan cheese

Salt and pepper to taste

Topping

1/4 cup cheddar cheese, grated

Directions

1. Combine all the casserole ingredients in a baking pan.

2. Top with the grated cheese.

3. Set your air fryer oven to bake.

4. Preheat your air fryer oven to 380 degrees F for 5 minutes.

5. Position the baking pan inside the air fryer oven.

6. Bake for 6 to 10 minutes or until cheese has melted.

Serving suggestion

Sprinkle with chopped green onion.

Tip

You can also add a little cayenne pepper to the casserole if you like.

Pesto Fish Fillets with Walnuts

 Preparation time
20 MINUTES

 Cooking time
10 MINUTES

 Servings
2

Ratings

Ingredients

2 salmon fillets

Salt and pepper to taste

2 tablespoons pesto sauce

1 tablespoon mayonnaise

1/4 cup walnuts, chopped

Directions

1. Season fish with salt and pepper.

2. Mix pesto and mayo.

3. Spread pesto sauce on top of fish.

4. Top with walnuts.

5. Place in the air crisper tray.

6. Choose air fry setting.

7. Place the fish in the air fryer oven.

8. Cook at 380 degrees F for 10 minutes.

Serving suggestion

Sprinkle with Parmesan cheese before serving.

Tip

Dry the fish thoroughly with paper towel before seasoning.

Thai Fish

Preparation time
5 MINUTES

Cooking time
10 MINUTES

Servings

Ratings

Ingredients

1 teaspoon soy sauce

2 teaspoons fish sauce

1 tablespoon oyster sauce

1 clove garlic, minced

1/2 tablespoon lime juice

1 tablespoon brown sugar

2 flounder fillets

Directions

1. Combine soy sauce, fish sauce, oyster sauce, garlic, lime juice and brown sugar in a bowl.

2. Brush both sides of fish with this mixture.

3. Add the fish fillets to the air fryer oven.

4. Set the air fryer oven to roast.

5. Cook at 370 degrees F for 5 minutes per side.

Serving suggestion

Sprinkle with thinly sliced fresh basil leaves.

Tip

Use low-sodium fish sauce and soy sauce.

Tuna and Avocado Croquettes

 Preparation time
5 MINUTES

 Cooking time
10 MINUTES

 Servings
4

Ratings

Ingredients

2 cups canned tuna flakes

1/4 teaspoon onion powder

1/2 avocado, pitted

2 tablespoons lemon juice

1/4 cup roasted almonds, chopped

1/2 cup breadcrumbs

Salt and pepper to taste

Directions

1. Combine all the ingredients in a bowl.

2. Form balls from the mixture.

3. Set your air fryer oven to air fry.

4. Place the tuna balls in the air crisper tray.

5. Cook at 380 degrees F for 8 minutes or until golden.

Serving suggestion

Serve with marinara dip.

Tip

You can also add chopped onion in the mixture.

Cod Fillet with Curry Butter

Preparation time
10 MINUTES

Cooking time
10 MINUTES

Servings
2

Ratings

Ingredients

1 tablespoon butter, melted

1/4 teaspoon curry powder

1/8 teaspoon paprika

Pinch garlic powder

Salt to taste

2 cod fillets

Directions

1. Combine butter, curry powder, paprika, garlic powder and salt in a bowl.

2. Coat cod fillets with this mixture.

3. Add cod fillets to the air fryer oven.

4. Set it to roast.

5. Cook at 360 degrees F for 4 to 5 minutes per side.

6. Drizzle with cooking liquid and serve.

Serving suggestion

Sprinkle with thinly sliced basil.

Tip

Add more curry powder if you like your fish spicier.

Cod with Soy Ginger Sauce

Preparation time
5 MINUTES

Cooking time
10 MINUTES

Servings
2

Ratings

Ingredients

1 tablespoon butter, melted
1-1/2 tablespoons rice wine
2 teaspoons honey
1 tablespoon soy sauce
2 cod fillets
1 tablespoon ginger, sliced thinly

Directions

1. Combine butter, rice wine, honey and soy sauce in a bowl.

2. Place the cod fillets on top of a foil sheet.

3. Sprinkle the ginger slices on top.

4. Pour the butter sauce over the fish.

5. Fold the foil to wrap the fish.

6. Pinch sides to seal.

7. Place in the air fryer oven.

8. Select air fry setting.

9. Cook at 360 degrees F for 10 minutes.

Serving suggestion

Garnish with cilantro.

Tip

You can also add sliced onions inside the packet.

Lemon Caper Fish Fillet

 Preparation time
5 MINUTES

 Cooking time
6 MINUTES

 Servings
2

Ratings

Ingredients

2 cod fillets
Salt and pepper to taste
1-1/2 tablespoons butter
1/2 teaspoon lemon zest
3 tablespoons lemon juice
1 tablespoon capers

Directions

1. Spray fish with oil.
2. Season with salt and pepper.
3. Place the fish inside the air fryer oven.
4. Choose air fry setting.
5. Cook at 360 degrees F for 3 minutes per side.
6. In a pan over medium heat, add the butter.
7. Once melted, stir in lemon zest, lemon juice and capers.
8. Simmer for 1 minute.
9. Transfer fish to a serving plate.
10. Pour sauce over the fish and serve.

Serving suggestion

Sprinkle with pepper.

Tip

Extend cooking time until fish is flaky.

Garlic Salt and Pepper Shrimp

Preparation time
5 MINUTES

Cooking time
6 MINUTES

Servings
8

Ratings

Ingredients

16 shrimp

2 teaspoons olive oil

1 teaspoon rice wine

Salt and pepper to taste

2 cloves garlic, minced

Directions

1. Combine all the ingredients in a bowl.

2. Set the air fryer oven to air fry.

3. Add the shrimp mixture to the air crisper tray.

4. Cook at 400 degrees F for 3 minutes per side.

5. Mix all ingredients together and let sit for 5 minutes.

Serving suggestion

Garnish with crispy garlic bits.

Tip

You can also use frozen shrimp for this recipe.

Sweet and Spicy Salmon

 Preparation time
5 MINUTES

 Cooking time
15 MINUTES

 Servings
4

Ratings

Ingredients

4 salmon fillets

1 tablespoon butter, melted

1/2 tablespoon chili powder

1/4 teaspoon paprika

2 tablespoons brown sugar

1 teaspoon cumin

Pinch cayenne pepper

Salt and pepper to taste

Directions

1. Brush both sides of salmon with butter.

2. Mix the remaining ingredients in a bowl.

3. Sprinkle salmon with the spice mixture.

4. Add salmon to the air fryer oven.

5. Choose roast setting.

6. Preheat your air fryer oven to 380 degrees F for 5 minutes.

7. For 6 minutes per side cook the salmon.

Serving suggestion

Let rest for 5 minutes before serving.

Tip

You can also brush with melted butter in between cooking.

Parmesan Fish Fillet

 Preparation time
10 MINUTES

 Cooking time
10 MINUTES

 Servings
2

Ratings

Ingredients

1/4 teaspoon paprika
1/2 teaspoon Italian seasoning
Salt and pepper to taste
2 fish fillets
1/4 cup Parmesan cheese, grated

Directions

1. Mix paprika, Italian herbs, salt and pepper in a bowl.

2. Season fish with the mixture.

3. Cover with Parmesan cheese.

4. Set the air fryer oven to bake.

5. Preheat it to 370 degrees F for 5 minutes.

6. Place the fish inside the air fryer oven.

7. Cook for 5 minutes per side.

Serving suggestion

Garnish with chopped green onion.

Tip

You can also add breadcrumbs to the breading.

Salmon Shioyaki

Preparation time
6 HOURS

Cooking time
10 MINUTES

Servings
4

Ratings

Ingredients

4 salmon fillets
2 tablespoons rice wine
4 teaspoons salt

Directions

1. Coat salmon with rice wine.

2. Let sit for 10 minutes.

3. Sprinkle with salt.

4. Place inside a sealable plastic bag.

5. Refrigerate for 6 hours.

6. Transfer salmon to the air crisper tray.

7. Choose air fry setting.

8. Cook the salmon at 400 degrees F for 4 to 5 minutes per side.

Serving suggestion

Garnish with lime wedges.

Tip

Dry salmon with paper towel before seasoning.

Meatless Dishes

Sriracha Cauliflower Stir Fry

Preparation time
5 MINUTES

Cooking time
30 MINUTES

Servings
4

Ratings

Ingredients

1 head cauliflower, cut into florets

1 tablespoon Sriracha

1-1/2 tablespoons tamari or gluten free tamari

3/4 cup onion white, thinly sliced

5 cloves garlic, minced

1 tablespoon rice vinegar

2 tablespoons olive oil

1/2 teaspoon coconut sugar

Directions

1. Combine all the ingredients in a bowl.

2. Place the mixture in the air fryer.

3. Set the oven in air fry mode.

4. Cook at 350°F for 30 minutes, shaking the pot every 10 minutes.

Serving suggestion

Garnish with scallions.

Tip

You can use other hot sauces instead of sriracha.

Roasted Potatoes and Asparagus

Preparation time
10 MINUTES

Cooking time
5 MINUTES

Servings
4

Ratings

Ingredients

4 new potatoes, cut and cooked

1 lb. asparagus, chopped

1 teaspoon dried dill

2 stalks scallions, chopped

Salt and pepper to taste

Directions

1. Combine the asparagus, scallions, and olive oil in a small bowl.

2. Select the roast function and cook the mixture at 350°F for 5 minutes.

3. Combine the mixture with the potatoes in a large bowl.

4. Season with dill, salt, pepper, and olive oil.

Serving suggestion

Garnish with fresh parsley.

Tip

Drain the potatoes well.

Sweet Potato Casserole with Marshmallows

Preparation time
20 MINUTES

Cooking time
12 MINUTES

Servings
4

Ratings

Ingredients

Mini marshmallows

3 cups sweet potatoes, cooked and mashed

1/2 cup pecans, diced

1/2 cup brown sugar

1 teaspoon vanilla extract

1/3 cup melted butter

1 teaspoon ground cinnamon

Salt and pepper to taste

Directions

1. Combine all the ingredients, except for the mini marshmallows.

2. Set the mixture on a greased casserole dish.

3. Arrange the mini marshmallows on top.

4. Select the bake function on your air fryer oven.

5. Bake at 320°F for 10 to 12 minutes.

Serving suggestion

Serve immediately.

Tip

Use gluten-free marshmallows.

Grilled Vegetable Platter

 Preparation time
15 MINUTES

 Cooking time
15 MINUTES

 Servings
6

Ratings

Ingredients

2 ears corn, quartered crosswise

8 oz. cremini mushrooms, halved

1 lb. asparagus, trimmed

1 lb. cherry tomatoes, stemmed

2 zucchinis, quartered lengthwise

3 tablespoons olive oil

Salt and pepper to taste

Directions

1. Grease the vegetables by brushing with olive oil.

2. Season with salt and pepper.

3. Set the oven in grill mode at medium heat.

4. Cook the vegetables, turning occasionally: mushrooms, asparagus, and mushrooms for about 3 or 4 minutes; corn and zucchini for 5 to 8 minutes.

5. Serve in a platter immediately.

Serving suggestion

Garnish with fresh basil leaves.

Tip

If available, season with Kosher salt and freshly ground black pepper.

Vegan Mini Lasagna

Preparation time
20 MINUTES

Cooking time
5 MINUTES

Servings
1

Ratings

Ingredients

2 lasagna noodles, halved and cooked

1/2 cup pasta sauce

1 cup baby spinach leaves, chopped

3 tablespoons zucchini

1 cup fresh basil leaves, chopped

1/4 cup tofu ricotta

Directions

1. Spread pasta sauce on a mini loaf pan.

2. Alternately layer the noodles with a mix of pasta sauce, spinach, zucchini, basil, and tofu ricotta.

3. Cover the loaf pan with aluminium foil.

4. Set the oven at 400°F on bake mode for 3 to 5 minutes.

Serving suggestion

Garnish with chopped parsley.

Tip

Use egg-free lasagna noodles.

Baked Zesty Tofu

Preparation time
30 MINUTES

Cooking time
10 MINUTES

Servings
4

Ratings

Ingredients

Sauce

2 tablespoons organic sugar
1/3 cup lemon juice
2 teaspoons arrowroot powder
1/2 cup water
1 teaspoon lemon zest

Tofu

1 tablespoon tamari
1 lb. extra-firm tofu, drained and pressed
1 tablespoon arrowroot powder

Directions

1. Incorporate all the sauce ingredients in a small bowl.

2. Coat the tofu with tamari, and then with arrowroot powder.

3. Set oven in bake function at 390°F.

4. Bake for 10 minutes, shaking halfway through.

5. Heat the tofu and sauce in a skillet over medium to high setting until the sauce thickens.

Serving suggestion

Serve with steamed rice and vegetables.

Tip

Use Meyer lemons to use less sugar.

Potato and Kale Nuggets

Preparation time
5 MINUTES

Cooking time
15 MINUTES

Servings
4

Ratings

Ingredients

1 teaspoon extra virgin olive oil

4 cups kale, chopped

1 clove garlic, minced

1/8 cup almond milk

2 cups potatoes, cooked

Salt and pepper to taste

Directions

1. Sauté the garlic and kale in oil for 2 or 3 minutes.

2. Mash the potato, adding milk, salt and pepper.

3. Combine the two mixtures, and then roll into 1-inch nuggets.

4. Cook on bake mode at 390°F for 12 to 15 minutes.

Serving suggestion

Serve with steamed rice or quinoa.

Tip

You may omit the olive oil, if desired.

Crispy BBQ Soy Curls

Preparation time
10 MINUTES

Cooking time
10 MINUTES

Servings
2

Ratings

Ingredients

1 cup soy curls
1 cup warm water
1 teaspoon vegetable broth
1/4 cup vegan barbecue sauce

Directions

1. Soak soy curls in warm water with vegetable broth for 10 minutes.

2. Drain and shred into a mixing bowl.

3. Cook on air fry setting at 400°F for 3 minutes.

4. Put back in mixing bowl and coat with barbecue sauce.

5. Air fry for another 5 minutes.

Serving suggestion

Serve with potato salad and collard greens.

Tip

In place of broth, you can use plain water.

Vegan Omelettes

Preparation time
10 MINUTES

Cooking time
8 MINUTES

Servings
3

Ratings

Ingredients

1/2 block of organic tofu

1/2 cup spinach, finely chopped

3 tablespoons nutritional yeast

1/2 teaspoon cumin

1/4 cup chickpea flour

1/2 teaspoon turmeric

1/4 teaspoon onion powder

1/4 teaspoon basil

1/4 teaspoon garlic powder

1 tablespoon apple cider vinegar

1/2 cup vegan cheese, grated

1 tablespoon water

Salt and pepper to taste

Directions

1. Puree all the ingredients in a processor, except for the spinach and cheese.

2. Combine the batter with spinach and cheese.

3. Make six omelettes into desired shape.

4. Cook on bake mode set at 370°F for 4 minutes on each side.

Serving suggestion

Serve in a sandwich.

Tip

Use a cookie cutter to shape your omelettes.

Cajun Fishless Filets with Pecan Crust

 Preparation time
5 MINUTES

 Cooking time
15 MINUTES

 Servings
3

Ratings

Ingredients

3/4 cup water

1 teaspoon Cajun seasoning blend

3/4 cup pecans, minced

3 tablespoons flax seed, ground

1/4 cup plus 2 tablespoons cornmeal, finely ground

10.1 oz. Gardein Golden Fishless Filets

Directions

1. Make batter by combining all the ingredients except for the filets.

2. Coat the filets with the batter.

3. Cook on roast mode at 390°F for 10 minutes.

4. Flip and roast for another 3 to 5 minutes.

Serving suggestion

Serve with rice and hot sauce.

Tip

You can check if the center is piping hot—meaning it's cooked—by poking with a fork.

BBQ Tofu Wings

Preparation time
15 MINUTES

Cooking time
20 MINUTES

Servings
4

Ratings

Ingredients

1 block extra firm tofu, cut in triangle wings

3/4 cup barbecue sauce

1/2 cup white wheat flour

1/4 cup cornstarch

Directions

1. Lightly brush the tofu with barbecue sauce.

2. Coat with cornstarch and flour.

3. Arrange on a lined baking sheet.

4. Cook using the bake setting at 350°F for 10 minutes.

5. Remove from air fryer and coat with sauce again.

6. Bake for another 10 minutes.

Serving suggestion

Top on a salad with a side of tahini dressing.

Tip

Use a rubber spatula when removing from air fryer to keep the tofu and coating intact.

Brussels Sprouts and Sweet Potatoes

 Preparation time
15 MINUTES

 Cooking time
20 MINUTES

 Servings
4

Ratings

Ingredients

4 cups Brussels sprouts, sliced lengthwise

6 cups sweet potato, diced

2 tablespoons low-sodium soy sauce

2 teaspoons garlic powder

Directions

1. Season the veggies with garlic powder.

2. Set the air fryer oven to roast mode at 400°F.

3. Roast the Brussels sprouts for 5 minutes.

4. Roast the sweet potatoes for 15 minutes.

5. Season the veggies with soy sauce, and then cook for another 5 minutes.

Serving suggestion

Serve with quinoa and peanut butter sauce.

Tip

Also try with tahini sauce.

Bacon Tofu

Preparation time
10 MINUTES

Cooking time
20 MINUTES

Servings
4

Ratings

Ingredients

1 block tofu, pressed and sliced
1 tablespoon olive oil
1/4 cup soy sauce
1 tablespoon liquid smoke
3 tablespoons balsamic vinegar
1 teaspoon garlic powder

Directions

1. Incorporate all the ingredients in a small bowl, except for the tofu.

2. Marinate the tofu with the mixture for 30 minutes.

3. Use the air fry setting of your oven.

4. Air fry at 400°F for 18 to 22 minutes.

Serving suggestion

Serve with grains or in a sandwich.

Tip

You can dice the tofu for salads and soups.

Sticky Orange Tofu

 Preparation time
30 MINUTES

 Cooking time
10 MINUTES

 Servings
4

Ratings

Ingredients

1 tablespoon tamari
1 tablespoon cornstarch
1 oz. extra-firm tofu, cubed

Sauce

1/3 cup orange juice
1 tablespoon pure maple syrup
2 teaspoons cornstarch
1/2 cup water
2 teaspoons cornstarch
1 teaspoon orange zest
1 teaspoon fresh ginger, minced
1 teaspoon fresh garlic, minced
1/4 teaspoon crushed red pepper flakes

Directions

1. Prepare the sauce by incorporating all the ingredients.

2. Coat the tofu with tamari, and then with cornstarch.

3. Use the air fry setting of your oven at 390°F.

4. Cook for 10 minutes, shaking halfway through.

Serving suggestion

Serve with steamed rice and vegetables.

Tip

You can also pair this with vegan noodles and fried rice.

Salted Broccoli with Lemon

 Preparation time
5 MINUTES

 Cooking time
15 MINUTES

 Servings
4

Ratings

Ingredients

Salt and pepper to taste
1.1 teaspoon garlic powder
2 tablespoons olive oil
Fresh lemon wedges
1 lb. broccoli

Directions

1. Drizzle broccoli with olive oil.

2. Toss in salt, pepper, and garlic powder.

3. Set the oven on air fry mode at 380°F.

4. Air fry for 12 to 15 minutes.

Serving suggestion

Serve with lemon wedges.

Tip

Flip and shake for at least three times while cooking.

Cheesy Brussels Sprouts with Garlic

 Preparation time
35 MINUTES

 Cooking time
25 MINUTES

 Servings
4

Ratings

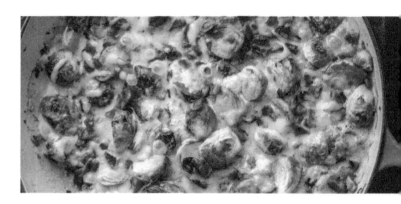

Ingredients

3/4 cup Parmesan cheese, grated

1-1/2 lb. Brussels sprouts, halved

4 cloves garlic, minced

1 tablespoon balsamic vinegar

2 tablespoons olive oil

Salt and pepper to taste

Directions

1. Add all the ingredients together, except for the Parmesan cheese.

2. Select the roast function on your air fryer oven.

3. Roast Brussels sprouts for 20 minutes.

4. Sprinkle cheese, and then roast for another 3 minutes.

Serving suggestion

Serve warm.

Tip

You may vegan cheese instead of Parmesan cheese.

Quinoa Pilaf with Garlic Tofu

Preparation time
10 MINUTES

Cooking time
15 MINUTES

Servings
4

Ratings

Ingredients

1 cup quinoa, cooked in vegetable broth

1 cup green peas, cooked

1 block extra-firm tofu, sliced and pressed

2 cloves garlic, minced

2 lemons, zested and juiced

Salt and pepper to taste

Directions

1. Make a marinade with garlic, lemon zest, lemon juice, salt, and pepper.

2. Marinate the tofu for 15 minutes.

3. Cook tofu on air fry setting at 370°F for 15 minutes.

4. Mix the quinoa pilaf, boiled green peas, and tofu.

Serving suggestion

You can serve warm or cold.

Tip

You can also try this with rice instead of quinoa.

Holiday Recipe

Crispy Roasted Chickpeas

Preparation time
5 MINUTES

Cooking time
10 MINUTES

Servings
3

Ratings

Ingredients

425 grams chickpeas, drained and patted dry

1 tablespoon olive oil

Salt to taste

Directions

1. Lightly grease the chickpeas with olive oil.

2. Add salt to taste.

3. In one layer spread the chickpeas on a sheeted baking pan.

4. Select the roast function in your air fryer oven.

5. Cook for 10 minutes at 390°F.

Serving suggestion

Put in a take-away container and snack away throughout the day. Also try them as toppings on your salad or soup.

Tip

Store in a paper bag or loosely covered container at room temperature for up to a week.

Crunchy Pasta Chips

 Preparation time
30 MINUTES

 Cooking time
10 MINUTES

 Servings
2

Ratings

Ingredients

1 tablespoon nutritional yeast

1-1/2 teaspoon Italian seasoning

Salt to taste

1 tablespoon olive oil

2 cups dry whole wheat bowtie pasta, cooked and drained

Directions

1. Combine the nutritional yeast, Italian seasoning, salt, and olive oil in a bowl.

2. Toss the pasta with the mixture.

3. Cook at 390°F for 10 minutes.

4. Shake the air fryer to cook evenly.

Serving suggestion

Enjoy as is or with your favorite dip.

Tip

Let the chips cool down completely to enjoy their maximum crunchiness.

Breaded Avocado Fries

Preparation time
10 MINUTES

Cooking time
10 MINUTES

Servings
4

Ratings

Ingredients

1 cup aquafaba

1/2 cup panko breadcrumbs

Salt to taste

1 Haas avocado, peeled and sliced

Directions

1. Put aquafaba into a shallow bowl.

2. In a separate container, mix the panko breadcrumbs and salt.

3. Dip the avocado slices in aquafaba, and then dredge them with the panko and salt mixture.

4. Arrange the slices in a single layer on a greased baking sheet.

5. Select the bake function on your air fryer oven.

6. Bake for 10 minutes at 390°F.

Serving suggestion

Serve immediately with a creamy sauce such as spicy mayo or ranch dressing.

Tip

For best results, use a slightly under-ripe avocado—neither too firm nor too soft.

Tomato and Cheese Pizza

 Preparation time
5 MINUTES

 Cooking time
10 MINUTES

 Servings
2

Ratings

Ingredients

12 inches pizza dough
1 teaspoon olive oil
1 tablespoon tomato sauce
Buffalo mozzarella

Directions

1. Spread the dough out to the size of two personal pan pizzas.

2. Lightly brush the dough with olive oil.

3. Spread a layer of tomato sauce.

4. Top with chunks of buffalo mozzarella.

5. Place the dough on a greased baking pan.

6. Select the bake function on your air fryer oven.

7. Bake at 375°F for 7 minutes.

Serving suggestion

Top with grated Parmesan cheese, basil, and pepper flakes.

Tip

The pizza will be piping hot so allow ample time for it to cool down before taking a bite.

Mozzarella Sticks

Preparation time
2 HOURS 15 MINUTES

Cooking time
10 MINUTES

Servings
2

Ratings

Ingredients

6 mozzarella sticks
3 tablespoons all-purpose flour
2 eggs, beaten
1 cup panko breadcrumbs

Directions

1. Freeze mozzarella sticks for at least 2 hours.

2. Set the flour, eggs, and panko in separate bowls.

3. Coat the mozzarella sticks in flour, and then dip them in egg, and then panko.

4. Dip the sticks in egg, and then panko again.

5. Arrange the sticks in a single layer on a baking sheet.

6. Select the bake function on your air fryer oven.

7. Bake at 400°F for 6 minutes.

Serving suggestion

Serve with warm marinara sauce.

Tip

Keep an eye while cooking, and do not let the cheese ooze out.

Cheesy Zucchini Chips

 Preparation time
10 MINUTES

 Cooking time
15 MINUTES

 Servings
4

Ratings

Ingredients

1 medium zucchini, thinly sliced
1 large egg, beaten
1 cup panko breadcrumbs
3/4 Parmesan cheese, grated
Cooking spray

Directions

1. Combine the panko and cheese.

2. In the beaten eggdip the zucchini slices, and then coat with the mixture.

3. Lightly grease with cooking spray.

4. Cook using the bake function on your air fryer oven at 350°F for 12 minutes.

Serving suggestion

You can use ranch dressing or marinara sauce for dipping.

Tip

Flip with tongs to cook evenly.

Sweet Potato Fries

Preparation time
5 MINUTES

Cooking time
20 MINUTES

Servings
4

Ratings

Ingredients

1/4 teaspoon paprika

1/2 teaspoon garlic powder

1/2 teaspoon fine sea salt

2 medium sweet potatoes, cut
into strips

1 tablespoon olive oil

Directions

1. Add all the ingredients except for the sweet potatoes and oil.

2. Coat the fries with oil and the mixture.

3. Set the air fryer oven to bake function at 380°F.

4. Cook for 18 minutes.

Serving suggestion

Garnish with parsley and serve with ketchup for dipping.

Tip

Keep an eye will cooking as the fries will brown at different rates depending on the size.

Three Ingredient Ravioli Bites

 Preparation time
5 MINUTES

 Cooking time
5 MINUTES

 Servings
2

Ratings

Ingredients

12 frozen ravioli

1/2 cup buttermilk

1/2 cup Italian breadcrumbs

Directions

1. Dip ravioli into the buttermilk.

2. Coat with breadcrumbs.

3. Cook using bake function at 400°F for 6 minutes or until golden brown.

Serving suggestion

Serve immediately with marinara sauce.

Tip

They can also be kept inside the fridge for up to 3 months.

Grilled Veggie Sandwich

 Preparation time
35 MINUTES

 Cooking time
10 MINUTES

 Servings
4

Ratings

Ingredients

1 tablespoon lemon juice
3 cloves garlic, minced
1/4 cup mayonnaise
1 small yellow squash, sliced
red onion, sliced
bell pepper, sliced
1 small zucchini, sliced
12 focaccia bread, sliced
1/2 cup crumbled feta cheese

Directions

1. Mix the lemon juice, garlic and mayonnaise; and then set aside in refrigerator.

2. Brush all the vegetables with olive oil.

3. Cook using grill function at high setting for 6 minutes, and then set aside.

4. Spread mayonnaise mix and cheese on the bread.

5. Grill for 2 to 3 minutes.

6. Transfer to plate and layer with the grilled veggies.

Serving suggestion

Top with alfalfa sprouts.

Tip

You may also enjoy it as an open sandwich.

Curled Zucchini Fries

 Preparation time
20 MINUTES

 Cooking time
10 MINUTES

 Servings
4

Ratings

Ingredients

1 cup panko breadcrumbs

1/2 cup Parmesan cheese, grated

1 teaspoon Italian seasoning

1 large zucchini, sliced using spiralizer

1 large egg, beaten

Directions

1. Mix the panko, cheese and Italian seasoning in a large resealable plastic bag.

2. Dip the zucchini in the beaten egg, and then put inside the bag with the mix to coat.

3. Use the bake function at 400°F for 10 minutes.

Serving suggestion

Serve with a zesty ranch dipping sauce.

Tip

Cook in batches for evenly crisped results.

Cinnamon Apple Chips

Ratings

Ingredients

2 medium apples, thinly sliced

Directions

1. Sprinkle the apple slices with cinnamon.

2. Put them in the air fryer basket. Weigh them down with a metal rack to prevent from flying around the basket.

3. Cook on air fryer mode at 300°F for 16 minutes.

4. Allow to cool and crisp for at least 5 minutes before serving.

Serving suggestion

Consume immediately once crisp.

Tip

Store in an airtight container for later. The chips will soften when exposed in the air for too long.

Zucchini Pizza Boats

Preparation time
5 MINUTES

Cooking time
7 MINUTES

Servings
6

Ratings

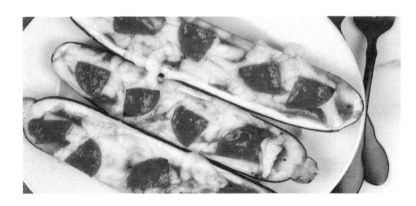

Ingredients

3 medium zucchinis, halved

1/2 cup pizza sauce

4 cup mozzarella cheese, shredded

Directions

1. Scoop out the center of the zucchinis to make boats.

2. Fill in the center with pizza sauce and cheese.

3. Cook in the air fryer at 350°F for 7 minutes.

4. Plate and enjoy.

Serving suggestion

Top with more cheese and serve warm.

Tip

You can tweak this recipe to load your boat with other fillings of your choice.

Roasted Shishito Peppers

Preparation time
10 MINUTES

Cooking time
5 MINUTES

Servings
4

Ratings

Ingredients

2 tablespoons olive oil

Salt and pepper to taste

8 oz Shishito peppers

Directions

1. Rub the Shishito peppers with olive oil, salt and pepper.

2. Cook on roast setting at 380°F for 5 to 7 minutes.

Serving suggestion

Enjoy by itself, or with cornbread.

Tip

You may also dice them to garnish your salad or soup.

Garlic Carrot Fingers

 Preparation time
10 MINUTES

 Cooking time
12 MINUTES

 Servings
4

Ratings

Ingredients

1 lb. carrot, peeled and cut
2 teaspoons garlic powder
Salt and pepper to taste
1 tablespoon olive oil

Directions

1. Coat the carrots by mixing all the ingredients.

2. Set the air fryer oven to roast mode at 390°F.

3. Roast for 10 to 12 minutes.

Serving suggestion

Garnish with parsley and cream cheese.

Tip

If you want a spicy version, just add ground cinnamon and chili powder into the mix.

Roasted Cauliflower

 Preparation time
5 MINUTES

 Cooking time
15 MINUTES

 Servings
4

Ratings

Ingredients

1 tablespoon sesame oil

Salt and pepper to taste

1 head cauliflower florets

3 teaspoons garlic powder

Directions

1. Season the florets with sesame oil, salt, pepper, and garlic powder.

2. Roast in your air fryer oven at 400°F for 15 minutes.

3. Flip the florets halfway through.

Serving suggestion

Garnish with grated parmesan cheese.

Tip

You may also coat with panko breadcrumbs.

Black Bean Burger

Preparation time
20 MINUTES

Cooking time
15 MINUTES

Servings
6

Ratings

Ingredients

16 oz. black beans, drained

1/2 cup corn kernels

1-1/3 cups rolled oats

¾ cup salsa

1/2 teaspoon garlic powder

1-1/4 teaspoons mild chili powder

1/2 teaspoon chipotle chili powder

1 tablespoon soy sauce

Directions

1. Except for the corn, blend all ingredients in a food processor.

2. Add the corn and refrigerate for 15 minutes.

3. Shape the mixture into patties.

4. Set the air fryer oven to bake mode at 375°F.

5. Bake for 15 minutes or until crispy.

Serving suggestion

Make a sandwich and serve with guilt-free air fryer fries.

Tip

Wrap the patties tightly and freeze for up to 3 months.

Crispy Falafel

Preparation time
10 MINUTES

Cooking time
15 MINUTES

Servings
6

Ratings

Ingredients

2 cups dried chickpeas, soaked

1 tablespoon chickpea flour

3/4 cup parsley, chopped

1 medium onion, diced

1/4 cup cilantro, chopped

2 cloves garlic, minced

2 teaspoons ground coriander

2 teaspoons cumin powder

1/2 teaspoon cayenne pepper

Salt and pepper to taste

Directions

1. Blend together all the ingredients slightly in a food processor to make a coarse mixture.

2. Shape the mixture into 1.5-inch balls.

3. Arrange in a single layer on a lined baking pan.

4. Cook on bake mode at 370°F for 15 minutes or until crispy and golden brown.

Serving suggestion

Serve with tzatziki sauce.

Tip

You may soak the chickpeas overnight for best results.

Lamb and Goat Dishes

Roasted Lamb Chops with Garlic and Rosemary

Preparation time
30 MINUTES

Cooking time
15 MINUTES

Servings
4

Ratings

Ingredients

2 tablespoons olive oil

1 tablespoon fresh rosemary, chopped

4 cloves garlic, minced

Pepper to taste

8 lamb chops

Salt to taste

Directions

1. Combine olive oil, rosemary, garlic, and pepper in a bowl.

2. Coat lamb chops with mixture.

3. Marinate for 30 minutes at room temperature.

4. Line your baking sheet with foil.

5. Season lamb chops with salt.

6. Position the baking pan inside the air fryer oven.

7. Choose bake function.

8. Bake at 425°F for 15 minutes.

Serving suggestion

Garnish with rosemary sprigs.

Tip

You can also marinate lamb chops overnight.

Lamb chops with Fennel and Orange Salad

 Preparation time
15 MINUTES

 Cooking time
30 MINUTES

 Servings
4

Ratings

Ingredients

6 garlic cloves, minced

2 garlic heads, sliced crosswise

1 teaspoon orange zest, grated

1 teaspoon red pepper flakes

1 cup white wine

2 tablespoons rosemary, finely chopped

2 tablespoons lemon juice

2 tablespoons olive oil

1 cup orange, sliced

6 to 8 lamb chops

1 fennel bulb, thinly sliced

Salt and pepper to taste

Directions

1. Score lamb with a sharp knife.
2. Season with salt and pepper.
3. Mix minced garlic, zest, olive oil, rosemary, and pepper flakes in a bowl.
4. Coat lamb with the mixture.
5. Place lamb in the baking pan together with garlic heads and wine. Cover with foil
6. Select the roast function.
7. Roast at 300°F for 30 minutes or until tender.
8. Mix fennel, orange slices, salt, and lemon juice in a bowl.
9. Serve with lamb chops.

Serving suggestion

Top lamb with rosemary.

Tip

Drizzle leftover juices over meat and salad.

Lamb Chops in Dijon Garlic

Preparation time
25 MINUTES

Cooking time
20 MINUTES

Servings
2

Ratings

Ingredients

8 pieces lamb chops
2 teaspoons Dijon mustard
1 teaspoon soy sauce
2 teaspoons olive oil
1 teaspoon cumin powder
1 teaspoon minced garlic
1 teaspoon cayenne powder
Salt to taste

Directions

1. Combine Dijon mustard, olive oil, cumin and cayenne powder, soy sauce, and garlic in a bowl.

2. Place lamb chops in a Ziploc bag together with the mixture.

3. Marinate for 30 minutes in the fridge.

4. Choose bake function.

5. Cook for 17 minutes at 350°F.

Serving suggestion

Add 3 minutes to the cooking time to make lamb chops well done.

Tip

You can also marinate the lamb chops overnight to save time.

Braised Lamb Shanks

 Preparation time
10 MINUTES

 Cooking time
2 HOUR 20 MINUTES

 Servings
4

Ratings

Ingredients

4 garlic cloves, crushed
1-1/2 teaspoon kosher salt
3 cups beef broth
4 sprigs of fresh rosemary
4 lamb shanks
2 tablespoons balsamic vinegar
Salt and pepper to taste

Directions

1. Rub lamb with salt, pepper, garlic, and olive oil.

2. Place in baking pan with rosemary.

3. Select roast function.

4. Roast for 20 minutes at 425°F.

5. Turn lamb halfway while roasting.

6. Add the vinegar and 2 cups of broth and switch to slow cook.

7. Slow cook at 250°F for 1 hour.

8. Add remaining cup of broth and slow cook for another hour.

Serving suggestion

Garnish with fresh rosemary sprigs.

Tip

Lamb is ready when the meat easily pulls from the bone.

Roasted Lamb with Cumin and Lemon Crust

 Preparation time
15 MINUTES

 Cooking time
25 MINUTES

 Servings
3

Ratings

Ingredients

1/2 cup breadcrumbs

1 egg, beaten

1 cloves garlic, grated

1 teaspoon cumin seeds

1/4 lemon rind, grated

1 teaspoon oil

1 teaspoon ground cumin

1.7 lb. rack of lamb, frenched

Salt

freshly ground black pepper to taste

Directions

1. Season lamb rack with salt and pepper.
2. Combine breadcrumbs, cumin seeds, garlic, ground cumin, oil, ½ teaspoon of salt, and lemon rind in a large bowl.
3. Dip the lamb in the egg then coat with the breadcrumb mixture until a crust is formed.
4. Arrange the lamb in the frying basket.
5. Choose the bake function.
6. Bake at 100°F for 25 minutes.
7. Switch to roast function.
8. Roast at 200°F for 5 minutes.
9. Remove from air fryer and cover with foil.
10. Leave alone for 10 minutes to rest before carving.

Serving suggestion

Serve with roasted vegetables or a fresh salad.

Tip

You can substitute Dijon mustard for the egg.

Lamb Rack with Potatoes and Yogurt Mint Sauce

Preparation time
10 MINUTES

Cooking time
20 MINUTES

Servings
2

Ratings

Ingredients

2 teaspoons fresh rosemary, chopped

1 teaspoon paprika

1 bunch asparagus

1-1/2 tablespoon olive oil

1 red bell pepper, cut into strips

1/2 lb. potatoes, cut into wedges

1 lb. lamb rack

Salt and pepper to taste

1/2 bunch mint, finely chopped

2/3 cup Greek yogurt

Directions

1. Season lamb with salt, pepper, and rosemary.
2. Coat potatoes with 1 tablespoon oil, paprika, and pepper.
3. Arrange lamb and potatoes in the pan.
4. Select roast function.
5. Roast for 15 minutes at 400°F.
6. Remove lamb and potatoes from air fryer and cover with foil for 10 minutes before carving.
7. Mix bell pepper and asparagus with the remaining oil.
8. Roast for 6 minutes at 300°F.
9. Mix yogurt with mint.

Serving suggestion

Serve lamb and vegetables with yogurt sauce.

Tip

You can also add Dijon mustard as seasoning before roasting.

Lamb Kebabs

Preparation time
5 MINUTES

Cooking time
10 MINUTES

Servings
3

Ratings

Ingredients

1 tablespoon extra-virgin olive oil

2 teaspoons cumin powder

1 lb. lamb fillet, cut into 1-inch pieces

Salt and fresh ground pepper to taste

Directions

1. Combine all the ingredients in a bowl.

2. Put 2 pieces of lamb onto 6-inch skewers.

3. Choose the air fry option.

4. Cook for 8 minutes at 400°F.

5. Flip halfway through the cooking time.

Serving suggestion

Serve with yogurt and mint sauce as finger food.

Tip

You can cook the lamb without the skewers and serve with pitta bread.

Spiced Lamb Chops with Garlic Yogurt sauce

Preparation time
30 MINUTES

Cooking time
10 MINUTES

Servings
4

Ratings

Ingredients

1/4 teaspoon allspice powder

1 teaspoon coriander, ground

2 teaspoons cumin, ground

2 cloves garlic, grated

3/4 teaspoon turmeric, ground

1/2 lemon, squeezed

1-1/2 cups Greek yogurt

Salt and pepper to taste

Cooking oil

8 lamb chops

Directions

1. Whisk together yogurt, garlic, lemon, salt, and pepper in a bowl.
2. Transfer 1/2 of the yogurt mixture to a small bowl and set aside.
3. Add the cumin, allspice, coriander, and turmeric to the yogurt mixture and set aside.
4. Season lamb chops with salt and pepper.
5. Coat lamb with spiced yogurt.
6. Leave at room temperature for 30 minutes.
7. Choose the air fry option.
8. Lightly spray the pan with oil and put lamb.
9. Air fry at 400°F for 3 minutes on each side.
10. Serve with the garlic yogurt mixture.

Serving suggestion

Serve with a fresh salad or herbed mashed potatoes.

Tip

Spray a light coating of oil halfway through or after flipping the lamb.

Air Fryer Feta and Lamb Frittata

Preparation time
5 MINUTES

Cooking time
15 MINUTES

Servings
4

Ratings

Ingredients

8 large eggs

1 garlic clove, grated

1 teaspoon lemon zest, grated

1/4 cup plain yogurt

4 oz. lamb, ground

1 teaspoon fresh lemon juice

2 scallions, thinly sliced

1/4 cup feta, crumbled

1 tablespoon tarragon leaves

2 cups baby kale

1 tablespoon za'atar

1/2 cup cilantro leaves

1/4 cup basil leaves, torn

Mild red pepper flakes

3 tablespoons olive oil

Salt

freshly ground black pepper to taste

Directions

1. In a bowl, mix 1 tablespoon oil, za'atar, garlic, 1/2 teaspoon lemon zest, lemon juice, and lamb. Season with salt and pepper.
2. Combine yogurt, eggs, scallions, feta, basil, tarragon, cilantro, and kale.
3. Whisk mixture and season with salt and pepper.
4. Select the air fry option in your air fryer oven.
5. Lightly coat pan with oil and add lamb mixture.
6. Set temperature to 350°F and cook for at least 2 minutes or until golden brown.
7. Pour in the egg mixture.
8. With a rubber spatula, pull in the sides until it has set evenly.
9. Switch to bake function.
10. Bake at 300°F F for 10 minutes.

Serving suggestion

Top with yogurt and garnish with lemon zest, pepper, and herbs.

Tip

Frittata is ready when the center wobbles when shaken.

Grilled Rosemary Jerk Lamb Chops

Preparation time
10 MINUTES

Cooking time
4 HOURS 10 MINUTES

Servings
6 - 8

Ratings

Ingredients

2 lb. lamb loin chops

1-1/2 tablespoons soy sauce

7 cloves garlic

1/3 cup scallions

1 sprig rosemary

1/2 Scotch bonnet chili

1/2 teaspoon allspice

1 medium yellow onion, chopped

Salt and pepper to taste

Directions

1. To make the marinade, blend soy sauce, garlic, onion, scallions, rosemary, chili, and allspice until smooth.

2. Coat and massage lamb chops with marinade.

3. Cover and chill for 4 hours.

4. Choose the grill option.

5. Grill lamb at 400°F for 11 to 14 minutes.

Serving suggestion

Garnish with rosemary sprigs.

Tip

Lamb can be marinated overnight.

Grilled Lamb Chops with Tzatziki Sauce

Preparation time
1 HOUR

Cooking time
10 MINUTES

Servings
2

Ratings

Ingredients

4 lamb loin chops

3 tablespoons olive oil

1/2 teaspoon red chili flakes

1 tablespoon fresh lemon juice

2 teaspoons dried dill

8 cloves garlic, minced

3/4 cup plain Greek yogurt

1/2 cup cucumber, minced

Kosher salt and pepper to taste

Directions

1. To create tzatziki sauce, whisk yogurt, 2 cloves minced garlic, 1 teaspoon dill, 1 tablespoon lemon juice, cucumber, salt, and pepper. Cover and chill.

2. Combine the remaining dill, garlic, lemon juice, chili flakes, and oil in a bowl to create the marinade.

3. Spice up the lamb with salt and pepper and place in a baking tray.

4. Coat lamb with the marinade and leave at room temperature for 1 hour.

5. Choose the grill function in your air fryer.

6. Grill lamb at 350°F for 4 to 6 minutes (medium-rare).

Serving suggestion

Spread tzatziki sauce on a platter and lay lamb chops on top.

Tip

A simple fresh green salad goes well with this dish.

Spiced Lamb Chops with Ginger Soy Sauce

Preparation time
2 HOURS 15 MINUTES

Cooking time
15 MINUTES

Servings
8

Ratings

Ingredients

8 lamb rib chops

1/3 cup scallions, finely chopped

3 tablespoons shallot, minced

2 tablespoons cilantro, minced

2 tablespoons ginger, minced

2 tablespoons garlic, minced

3 tablespoons oyster sauce

1 tablespoon sugar

2 tablespoons light soy sauce

Steamed Bok choy

Salt and pepper to taste

Red and yellow bell peppers, julienned

Scallions, julienned

Directions

1. Combine oyster sauce, soy sauce, oil, cilantro, sugar, garlic, shallot, and ginger.
2. Add lamb chops and leave to marinate for 2 hours at room temperature.
3. Choose grill function in your air fryer.
4. Place lamb in tray and season with salt and pepper.
5. Grill chops at 400°F for 6 minutes.
6. Transfer to a platter and cover with foil.
7. Let sit for 10 minutes.
8. Pour marinade into the pan and cook for 8 minutes or until it is reduced to create the sauce.

Serving suggestion

Arrange steamed Bok choy in the plate and put lamb over together with julienned peppers and scallion. Serve with the sauce from the marinade.

Tip

To reduce preparation time, marinate the lamb overnight, and keep in the fridge.

Spicy Lamb with Lentils and Herbs

Preparation time
20 MINUTES

Cooking time
15 MINUTES

Servings
4

Ratings

Ingredients

1/2 lb. ground lamb

2 garlic cloves, thinly sliced

1/2 teaspoon cumin seeds

3/4 cup plain Greek yogurt

1 teaspoon crushed red pepper flakes

1/2 cucumber, chopped

1/4 cup fresh parsley

1/2 cup fresh cilantro, chopped

1-1/2 cups French green lentils

1 tablespoon vegetable oil

Kosher salt and pepper to taste

Flatbread and lemon wedges

Directions

1. Season lamb with salt and pepper.
2. Place lamb on the baking sheet.
3. Choose the air fry option.
4. Air fry for 350°F for 5 minutes.
5. Break apart lamb and add red pepper flakes, cumin, and garlic.
6. Cook for 2 more minutes and set aside.
7. Season lentils with salt and pepper.
8. Put lentils in the baking pan and cook until brown for 6 minutes.
9. Add the lamb back and mix well.
10. Remove from heat and add parsley, cucumber, and cilantro.

Serving suggestion

Spread yogurt on the plate and put the lamb on top. Serve with the flatbread and lemon wedges.

Tip

Garnish with fresh parsley and cilantro leaves.

Salt and Pepper Lamb

Preparation time
25 MINUTES

Cooking time
15 MINUTES

Servings
4

Ratings

Ingredients

1-1/2 lb. lamb rump

4 oz. rice flour

3-1/2 oz. plain flour

3 egg whites

2 zucchinis, thinly sliced

1 red capsicum, sliced into strips

1 green capsicum, sliced into strips

Directions

1. Cut lamb into thin stripsacross the grain.
2. Combine flours in a bowl and season with salt and pepper.
3. Whisk eggs in a separate bowl.
4. Dip strips of lamb in the egg then onto the flour individually.
5. Lightly coat a baking tray with oil.
6. Select the air fry option.
7. Air fry lamb for 3 to 4 minutes at 350°F.
8. Set aside lamb.
9. In the same tray, arrange the capsicums and zucchinis.
10. Air fry for 2 to 3 minutes until tender and has light charring.

Serving suggestion

Serve lamb with charred vegetables, lime wedges, and mayonnaise

Tip

You can also add freshly chopped onions as garnish.

Barbecue Lamb Cutlets

 Preparation time
30 MINUTES

 Cooking time
40 MINUTES

Servings
4

Ratings

Ingredients

2 cups tomato ketchup

1/2 cup white vinegar

2 teaspoons Tabasco sauce

3 teaspoons Worcestershire sauce

1/2 cup brown sugar

1 onion, fincly chopped

2 teaspoons mild mustard

4 large potatoes, cut into wedges

3-1/2 oz. sour cream

3 tablespoons vegetable oil

2 tablespoons mint, chopped

Salt and pepper to taste

16 small lamb chops

Directions

1. To make the marinade, combine onion, ketchup, vinegar, Worcestershire sauce, tabasco sauce, and sugar.
2. Soak lamb cuts in the marinade for 1 hour in the refrigerator.
3. Mix oil with salt and pepper.
4. Coat potatoes with the oil mixture.
5. Choose the air fry option.
6. Air fry at 400°F for 25 minutes until crispy.
7. Set aside potatoes once cooked.
8. Take out lamb and place it in the baking tray.
9. For 15 minutes Air fry at 350°F.

Serving suggestion

Place 4 pieces of lamb on each plate. Serve with potato wedged topped with sour cream and garnished with mint leaves.

Tip

You can marinate the lamb overnight to save time.

Conclusion

Dear Reader,

I can tell you in all confidence that I have tested all the recipes above and have been satisfied not only with their excellent success but also with the performance of Emeril, without which I would not have achieved such results! That's why I have poured into this book all the experience and expertise accumulated during my culinary experiments, and that's why I am convinced I can help you solve many problems. At least in the kitchen!

;)

So go ahead and experiment with your Emeril Lagasse air fryer, and remember: your imagination is the first and most valuable ingredient in any recipe!

Ciro

Made in the USA
Las Vegas, NV
05 November 2023